Just Once, No More

On Fathers, Sons, and Who We Are
Until We Are No Longer

Charles Foran

Alfred A. Knopf Canada

PUBLISHED BY ALFRED A. KNOPF CANADA

Copyright © 2023 Charles Foran

www.penguinrandomhouse.ca

Library and Archives Canada Cataloguing in Publication
Title: Just once, no more : on fathers, sons, and who we are
until we are no longer / Charles Foran.
Names: Foran, Charles, 1960- author.
Identifiers: Canadiana (print) 20220266239 |
Canadiana (ebook) 20220266360 | ISBN 9781039001053 (hardcover) |
ISBN 9781039001060 (EPUB)
Subjects: LCSH: Foran, Dave. | LCSH: Foran, Charles, 1960-—Family. |
LCSH: Fathers and sons—Canada—Biography. | LCSH: Parent and adult
child—Canada—Biography. | LCSH: Aging parents—Canada—Biography. |
LCSH: Fathers—Canada—Biography. | LCGFT: Biographies.
Classification: LCC HQ755.86 .F67 2023 | DDC 306.874/2092—dc23

Text design: Lisa Jager
Jacket design: Lisa Jager
Image credits: Pobytov/Getty Images

Printed in Canada

10 9 8 7 6 5 4 3 2 1

Penguin
Random House
KNOPF CANADA

There are as many shipwrecks as there are men.

—JOSEPH CONRAD

PART
ONE

I

My father once met a bear in the bush. He was following a path at dusk, ten miles in from the road, a Winchester 44-40 cradled in his arms. Around him the day was draining, and the moon through trees cast shapes onto the ground. Even so, he was in no hurry. The shapes reminded him of the lampshade in his childhood bedroom, the one featuring silhouettes of forest creatures—a rabbit and a deer, a moose with antlers. A bulb inside the shade had thrown the images onto the bedroom wall, making the boy wonder if he was awake and gazing at a movie screen or asleep and dreaming that he was in a forest. As well, there were the early spring scents of pine needles and running sap, the earth newly out from under snow. The scents started him thinking about his mother. Her perfume, yes, but more the smell on her breath and of the liquid in the glass beside her, which he had sipped and found so sweet, and so bitter.

He was walking back to camp from town, having spent the afternoon with his new gal. She was a beauty, a real keeper, and hiking six hours each direction to court her made sense, at least to his twenty-two-year-old body. He had walked further before, and for less happy reasons. The previous winter, the camp cook, an alcoholic who had taken the job to avoid taverns, had overdosed on a crate of vanilla extract. As foreman, my father had to first walk into town to report the death and then return the next morning with a police officer. They'd tied the corpse to a sled and hauled it back together, crossing the lake on snowshoes to save time.

Today's trip was much easier. He was thinking of the girl in town, and of his mother drinking her drink, and of the lamp in his bedroom all those years ago, when he came upon the bear. More accurately, in the miasma of dusk-into-dark and its hothouse of smells, he brushed up against the animal. Both parties were startled. My father should have heard, and above all inhaled, the presence earlier; the bear, too, ought to have sensed another being. As it was, they sideswiped each other on the path, and reacted predictably. Nostrils flooding with the musk of a male in heat, my father fell onto his backside, fumbling the rifle. The bear sat on its haunches and roared, spraying a gooey wash. It was about to drop back down onto all fours—and onto him—when my father regained control of the 44-40 and raised the barrel. Aiming for the gut, he shot the bear's head instead, blowing it half off. Blood, brain and bone splattered over his face, hair and jacket. The creature lurched, and for a second he worried it would topple forward— another way for a man to end up dead in the bush.

The bear fell sideways and landed with a thump, emitting an even more overpowering stink—of fear and death—along with a peculiar high whistle. Though the body twitched, my father knew the life had gone out. Laying the rifle on the ground, the barrel hot, he squatted next to the corpse for a minute, covering his mouth at the smell but not wiping his face of bone, brain or blood. He was in shock. He was thinking, too, about the kill. My father had hunted deer, rabbit and raccoons for their meat. He'd eaten too many grouse during long spells in the bush, killing them with his ax when they popped their heads up from the snow and then boiling the carcasses with rice and seasoning. Twice he had tried bear, neither the result of his own shooting, and found the meat greasy and hard to digest.

Something else kept him squatting next to the corpse in the gathering dark and cold, ten miles from town or camp. It was the whistle the animal had emitted from its shattered snout. In the final intake of breath, the last exhale, my father had detected a sigh. He knew he wasn't mistaken; he couldn't make such a notion up. A sigh of recognition? Sadness? Spring had finally bloomed, and the forest was coming alive. Might the bear have been off to meet a female—hence the distracted state—and make a baby, and then look after his new mate, the lovers eventually basking in the long days of summer, fish in the rivers and berries on the bushes? That sounded all right. That sounded like a life.

Not now, though. Not ever.

My father caught himself. Without another glance he rose and resumed hiking, only now back *into* town, three hours at a trot, never out of breath. Along with a flashlight, he used the brilliant harvest moon flickering through branches as aid, occasionally checking his compass. He also sang Hank Williams tunes to keep himself calm and warn away other forest creatures, remembering how he had jitterbugged with his new gal to "Hey, Good Lookin'" and "Jambalaya" in the Harmonic Hotel the other Saturday night. Williams, his favorite musician, had died the year before, aged just twenty-nine. Of booze and pills—or so it was said. What a shame.

During his four years in the bush, my father had driven a Jeep into a lake—the brakes failed; he'd bailed in the nick—and gone snow-blind, huddling in a tent for days until he'd regained his sight. He had exchanged gunfire with a rival, hearing and feeling a bullet brush past his ear, and survived two months off the grid, not seeing a single other human, following logging roads and Indian trails. In town he had brawled in taverns, using a beer bottle as a weapon, and succumbed to pneumonia, sweating it out in a hotel serving as a sick ward. Now he had survived a bear in the bush. He was thin, quick and coiled, and almost never afraid; he could survive a lot more.

And the girl, a volunteer nurse during the pneumonia outbreak, *was* a keeper. Her name was Muriel Fallu. She was second youngest of fourteen children born to a mill worker in Blind River, a town along the north channel of Lake Huron. A dozen of the kids survived, eleven of them girls. When my father met her, Muriel was twenty and had lately nursed her exhausted mother through her final months. My father proposed to her, and she accepted, on the condition he find work in town. They married in 1955. Two years later, the couple moved south to Toronto, where he landed a job building bomb shelters for the army. They bought a house in the suburbs and made three kids of their own.

My father was rust haired and cobalt eyed, shy of smile and more so of soul. Not tall, he traveled low to the ground, legs muscular and gut ballooning. He was born, he liked to declare, David Aloysius Horatio Debussy Charles Patrick Joseph Michael Lloyd Morton Foran, a faux-pomp run-on of names he claimed as his ancestry. All the while, he was playing a hand closer—by his own reading—to that of an orphan, dealt no face cards, forever obliged to bluff. He'd had parents, but they, it seemed, never had him. Certainly not his developmental needs, not his emotional welfare. Nor his back.

One parent he eventually lost directly to alcohol, and the other indirectly to war. But both lived for decades into his adulthood, estranged equally from each other as they were from their only son, and so my father struggled most days of his life with wounds he could not readily identify, let alone heal. His eyes could be laughing and sorrowful all at once, and his manner shift so abruptly from bluster to brooding that a sentence begun in one mood might finish in another. He trusted exactly a single human to love him regardless, not to abandon him too—giving over that trust to Muriel Fallu, now Muriel Foran, astounded and humbled and, I often sensed, perpetually grateful. It took me nearly forty years to read in his gaze uncertainty about being loved rather than anger at being alive, and to accord the gentleness beneath his bluster the stature of bravery, given that bad hand.

The young man in the bush, hunting and shooting, falling through ice and going snow-blind, was the immediate result of a disaster of a childhood. Later, the more drawn-out consequence was the unlikely shopping-center executive and even less probable suburban patriarch, too complex and solitary to befriend the neighbors. Even into his late sixties, retired to country living, my father showed more jagged edge than smooth surface, once approaching a stranger half his age who had insulted his daughter and decking him with a fist. Anger circulated within his body the way freckles covered his skin—everywhere, and lit by some eternal flame. Not only did he never get over what had happened to him as a boy, he didn't try. Men usually didn't try back then. Their families just had to deal.

In 2015, Dave Foran, age eighty-three, took sick for good. That same year his eldest son, age fifty-five, began this account.

The need to write about my father came as a surprise. I had not written much about him before and had plenty else on my mind, and in my computer. But once he began his final and, it turned out, slow decline, I started wanting to track it, and him, more closely—not as a hunter but as an investigator, possibly an interrogator as well. At the outset I could boast clear and honorable motives. To help lift an inchoate burden from his shoulders. To absolve him of the shame that composed much of that lifelong weight. To reassure him that he was loved. To get him to explain why he could never be close to anyone except Muriel.

How I wished all this for my father. And for me. But mostly—I was certain—for him.

2

During the winding down of my father's life, I also began tracking an uneasiness within myself. The disquiet was new, and so out of character that I could not at first put a name to what I appeared to be experiencing. Until I could: late into the middle of my own lifespan, sadness took hold of my being. I should probably write "a" sadness, or "a different kind" of sadness, and not use qualifiers like "appeared to be." Only that wasn't the sensation, or the condition, and I wanted to say so, never mind how uncomfortable I was with such language.

The truth was, I hadn't internalized sadness much until then. I had felt sad on occasions, naturally enough, not being a rock in a stream. Never for long, though, and never, I suspected, the way other more sentient humans did—as an awareness permanently informing how one lived and loved and under-stood experiences, especially loss. In its mature form, sadness was an emotional state I could barely claim familiarity with.

I felt the same about boredom, but ascribed that to a rest-less, eliding intelligence, combined with a puppy keenness for any fresh object to chew on. I was okay with never being bored, nor imagining I could be. Boredom is about negotiating with time, and my negotiation was straightforward: I didn't have enough of it, and wouldn't, ever.

Not "getting" sadness was different. It had seemed a personal failing, the strategy of someone who could manage only the shallow end of adulthood, even as he declared himself a capable swimmer who happened not to care to venture into the deep. I was lucky and blessed, crudely capable and lazily entitled, and aware that others had faced, and were facing, far greater challenges than I, although they might reject these designations as my baggage, not theirs. Also, I had known loss. People I loved had died. Important relationships failed or faded. Favorite pets were killed or put down. Thrilling experiences ended and treasured moments passed, never to reoccur.

And what about the colossal, overriding sadness of mortality? Why hadn't I, like so many, been almost incapacitated by it? When I gazed up at a clear night sky, at stars glimmering without casting light, or studied a grain of sand on my fingertip, I never discerned God or eternity or intimations of an afterlife. I just saw sky and sand. I just saw myself seeing these things.

How pitiful, not to believe in a reality beyond what is here; to believe only in what is visible, only in who I am, or think I am, at this moment. To others, faith appeared a sustaining joy, while faithlessness, its presumed opposite, was an ineffable sorrow. For me, faith was a nonstarter, but I felt neither joy nor sorrow over this, and I could not be persuaded, or perhaps humbled, otherwise.

A friend liked to tell an anecdote about his older brother. Alone among his large family, the brother, a property developer, had not shown the slightest interest in the big questions: Is there a God? Who are we? How should we conduct ourselves? Such questions irritated him, as if they were a waste of his time, even, somehow, of his money. One day my friend asked his brother if he had never heard of Socrates' dictum that the unexamined life isn't worth living. His sibling had not. He gave it some thought, but quickly became exasperated—with himself or, more likely, Socrates—and complained that he needed to be somewhere ten minutes ago, and his kid brother was making him late. Before he hurried away, though, he did voice an opinion about whether the unexamined life isn't worth living. "Bullshit," the brother said.

Now I wondered: Had this been my false front for decades, pretending I hadn't the leisure to understand deep sadness, calling "bullshit" instead?

Then sadness kindly stopped for me.

I can assign a month and year: October 2015. My father was in hospital with a kidney infection, and I was driving up from the city to visit him. It was a Saturday, the air crisp and the light honey-hued, oak and maple trees in flame. I was traveling country roads and tracking my progress using a private network of beacons. These were the barns a generation or two beyond purpose and, increasingly, repair. They dotted the landscape, some distressed but still standing, timber walls quaking and roofs askew, others with one side down and top

caved in. A few were full-on ruins, stone or concrete founda-
tions supporting piles of wood, funeral pyres awaiting a torch.
It was the ruined barns that interested me the most.

Unbidden, a list formed in my mind as I drove, complete
with a title. I pulled over in front of a farm and keyed it into
my phone.

WHY OLDER PEOPLE GET SAD:

- Death of loved ones
- Loss of driving purpose: mating, children, career
- Ebbing of once-vital relationships
- Overall feeling of diminishment—intellectual,
  creative, sexual
- Health issues
- Loneliness
- Pattern recognition in nature—i.e., mortality
- Tired of same old self
- Less and less taste to food
- Inability to find/feel/experience God

What a curious impulse, I thought to—and about—myself.
Oddly emphatic. And plaintive, as if I had forgotten to wear
clothes that morning and was sitting naked behind the
wheel. Putting the phone down, I carried on to the hospital,
slowing along the way to admire the trees in autumn beauty
and the barns in collapse. The smell of a fire, a pyre, was not
yet in the air.

Only in the hospital parking lot did I realize I hadn't examined my personal claim to the items on the list. I opened the document back up. For sure, numbers Two and Three resonated in general, along with an anxious nod toward number Four. Number Nine was goofy and made no sense (although I did over-spice my own food and used too much salt). As for the remaining six concerns, they were not my own. Or not much mine. Or not yet.

I climbed out of the car, groaning after the long drive and testing my bad knee on the asphalt before committing the weight. Already I was checking my watch to see how long I could visit before needing to return home; already I was telling myself to leave irritation and impatience outside my father's room. Why irritated? Why impatient? Maybe I had kept something off the list, and the missing item was nagging at me? I couldn't think what that might be.

Still, I had laid out ten reasons older people get sad as fast as I could key them into the phone. How to explain such ease in producing such uneasy thoughts? I couldn't. Enough self-examination for today, I decided. Better go see my sick dad.

3

Inside the enclosure, it is hushed. Sounds and sensations that assailed you for the past hour—the whorl of wind and slap of rain, the crash of waves against rock—have receded, as though the earth has drawn a breath and is holding it. Yes, you are cold and wet, hands purple and lips, you imagine, blue. And yes, part of you wishes to be back in the village guesthouse, by the turf fire, the flames leaping up.

But you are here instead, in a place where the earth holds its breath.

You are inside a Neolithic fort called Dún Aengus. The inner sanctum is protected by stone ramparts. Ten feet high and four feet across, the ramparts block the force of most of the elements. The floor is of granite, striated with tufts of grass, reminding you of an abandoned church—another hushed, reverent space. Didn't churches once shelter terrified villagers threatened with pillage and murder? And didn't those structures generally fail to arrest the violence? History, you decide, is human-on-human mayhem, while nature looks on in puzzlement.

But something else is happening at Dún Aengus. You are nineteen years old, and, having no clue what it might be, resolve to find out. The far wall of the enclosure, half a football field away, is especially alluring. It is composed partly of ocean that has ascended some improbable slope to meet land. The far wall is made up of sky as well, doming the island and touching down along this seam. Curious. Beautiful too, offering variances of blue: powdery and luminous higher up, darker with shadows below.

Off you go, seeking the spot where the hues join. Ten paces you cover, then twenty, the blues further clarifying, alongside the return of sound. You detect a watery roar, loud and in surround. You feel a breeze pushing and pulling at your torso. And you can't miss the squawk of birds—seagulls in the distance, except that you spot several of them just ahead, hovering over the ground.

The seagulls are airborne, wings wide and calls piercing, but not in the sky above. They idle in the sky below, poised within the now-dissolved blue. Very strange, you admit. Lucky that the ground remains beneath your feet.

You put your hands out—to join, to touch the seam. In so doing, you step off a cliff, a drop of four hundred feet.

Or, you almost do.

Your body registers extreme danger with a second to spare. Collapsing onto your knees will not be enough; the momentum will carry you over. You must rear up and windmill your arms. Feeling earth, but only under your heels, you will need to crumble sideways and then onto your back, not your stomach. Your back will be met by granite, your stomach by air.

The direction you choose is the correct one. You crack your left cheek on stone; your vision jumps and rolls vertically, a TV screen that has lost its sync. And you lie there, gaze now occluded by pain. Your left arm actually dangles over the ledge, an anchor pulling into the deep. Using your heels, you shimmy an inch to the right, and then another. Finally, that stray arm is also on land. Only then do you raise it to your forehead. Fingertips come back bloody, and you taste salt.

Your first cogent thought, beyond disbelief at your stupidity? Lines from a poem you learned in your final term of high school. "I'm Nobody! Who are you?" Emily Dickinson wrote. "Are you—Nobody—Too?"

Then you shimmy some more, also in the correct direction, and the danger passes. A voice calls out. Not God or your archangel: a couple further along the ledge, on their bellies, heads over the drop. How did you not notice them before? The woman asks if you are okay. "Watch," the man says. He crawls backwards, draws up to his knees, stands. "Easy," he adds.

You try explaining your mistake. "The two blues . . . The sea and sky. The way they came together . . ."

"You're bleeding," the woman says.

After that, you do as the man suggests. Chin over the ledge, spray across your face, Atlantic swells churning your stomach. Those seagulls too, floating not so far away, calling *ha ha ha ha*. You hear *told you so, told you so*.

The bliss lasts maybe a minute. Then another thought—an image, sprung from behind the eyes—jolts you. On either side of you villagers hurl themselves off the ledge. Women with children held to their chests, children together, opting to be swallowed by ocean rather than violated by men. Eyes alarmed. Mouths screaming, no sound coming out. Once again, your visual field is disrupted, and begins to flicker and roll. Also, there is a clanging sound, as though cliff and coastline are cymbals being struck together within your head. It is almost unbearable. Likewise awful is how you can suddenly feel, if not hear, the terror of the villagers as they brush by, along with—admit it—a pull to join them. Their bodies plummeting through the cool, wet air. Their minds, about to be set free. They are hurtling into the seam, and the seam—you sense, on their behalf; telling, you suppose, their forgotten tales—is opening. For them. For you. For Nobody.

So, what is Dún Aengus? You have the barest inkling, being young and fit and destined not to die that afternoon. Returning to the guesthouse and the fire, you think of a line from an anthology of Irish poetry you have been carrying in your rucksack. "I am the wind on the sea," a poet wrote in the tenth century. "I am the wave of the sea."

Is that what the poet truly wanted—to become the wind, the wave? Is that what you briefly wished for along that precipice?

Days later, on the flight home, you think: your father will love this story. He will get Dún Aengus, get the wild, reckless thrill of it. By extension, he will get you better too, both who you already are, and who you are still becoming. Soon after landing, you tell him a barebones version of what happened. Sheepish and unsure, you wait for him to ask more, to offer to puzzle it out with you—all those crazy ideas and intimations. He does not.

4

My father shed sixty pounds during his initial hospital stay. He was there a total of almost three months, sometimes in a room with other patients, but often in isolation, due to a string of infections. He claimed never to be hungry, blaming the medications and lack of activity. He also claimed he could only eat the food prepared by my mother, his wife-of-sixty-years, in their home, at their kitchen table. He survived on cookies and sweetened coffees smuggled by visitors, and the pounds came off. The day I finally registered his diminished size, my first impulse was to ask the nurses if they had switched him to a larger bed. My second was to force-feed him the fatty foods he once loved—shepherd's pie, liver and onions.

I did neither. I reminded myself that he was alive, that this was a happy surprise. Earlier in the fall, he'd had an emergency operation on his kidneys. Family was summoned bedside. Doctors warned us he might not survive. I found him on a gurney in a corridor, waiting for the surgery, and held his hand. Anguish altered his face and a pulse bounced in his wrist. "Why aren't they letting me go?" he said. "I want to go." Hearing that, I tried saying good-bye with my eyes. But later, the doctor told us how hard Dave Foran had fought on the operating table. "One tough hombre," he said.

Tough hombres, especially those confined to hospitals, kept fighting trim. The next visit, I sat beside his bed watching him drawbridge the pajama bottoms he wore beneath the gown, snapping the fabric against his deflated tummy.

"I feel so much better," my father said. "Look better too."

"You do," I said.

"*You* don't."

"Okay."

"You look tired. Pissed off. Could lose a few pounds," he said, snapping the pajama bottoms again. "Maybe more than a few . . ."

He was right, in his usual cutting way. "The older I get," I said, "the more I look like you."

"You and Mike are definitely brothers," he said of my younger sibling.

"So I'm told."

"He could also drop some weight."

"I'll let him know."

"And Debbie . . ." he began to say of our older sister.

I redirected the conversation. "Everyone says Debbie looks like Ruthie," I said of our grandmother, his mother. Only there was no "everyone," and although there *had* been a Ruthie Foran, I knew her mostly from photos, not memories.

My father frowned. We both paused in this doorway, the room beyond it dark and windowless. "Your hair," I said, stepping back, "it's like it was twenty years ago. The freckles as well," I added, touching his arm.

"How about that," he said.

It was true. Rust-colored hairs had recently reappeared on his head, after a decade of gray and white. I had noted as well the return of pigment to his skin, especially along his forearms. That was a private and near-forgotten thrill. My father's forearms were maps that his eldest son, in childhood, had loved to study. Like the front and rear flaps of a picture book, the maps depicted a dense archipelago of islands with narrow passageways in between. Adventures abounded in these waters. There were false tributaries and dead-end creeks, stiletto rocks and shoals, rapids and waterfalls that showed on no charts. Strewn throughout the archipelago were the wrecks of ships that had failed to navigate safe passage. Few made it, and for every shipwreck visible, another dozen lay at the bottom of the sea.

As a boy I had sat in my father's lap or next to him, outlining routes with my fingers. I told myself stories of heroic captains and crews, nasty pirates and octopuses, waves cresting into water walls and masts snapping under the strain. Launching from his elbow, I passed through the same gateway of freckles and proceeded south toward his wrist. He had not minded, except to occasionally complain that it tickled and pull away with a "ha ha," making me kick my feet and laugh. Nor, as best I can recall, did he wonder what I was doing. This, despite my sometimes asking for a nautical term and, I imagine, muttering bits of that day's adventure aloud.

The freckles eventually receded, along with my interest in, or even memory of, mapping his arms. Now the archipelagos had re-emerged, emitting the low, dense glow of a fire brought back from ash with a bellows.

His eyes had not staged a similar rebound. Once an intense, oceanic blue, Dave Foran's stare had functioned in two modes. One bore a hole into the other person, sure as a bullet, and made men, in particular, alert and wary, ready to duck. The other was sparkle-mode, rendering his often-awkward mischief—tilts into goofiness, a breathtaking lack of tact—harmless and endearing. Many women had liked the sparkle, reading vulnerability not far below.

But now the blue too had washed out, paint poured into a rushing stream, and the irises had clouded over. He ceased holding eye contact with other people for more than a glance, preferring to look past, or look right through, as though one of you wasn't there. Not really. Not any longer.

Registering that faraway gaze partway into his first pro-longed stay in hospital, and finding it incongruent with the trimmer waistline and blazing freckles, I started driving the two hours north from the city as often as I could, uncertain of how much time we—he, more precisely—had left. I also began using those barns along the route to prepare for our conversations. These would be meaningful exchanges. We would get some-where, finally, before it was too late. Only one subject truly interested me: his family and childhood. By my count, four ruined barns required our excavation. They had names and narratives—Charlie Foran, Ruthie Foran, Shirley Foran, Barb Norton—but, equally, they were archetypes. The imperious father. The fragile mother. The intruder second wife. The co-damaged sibling. Complexity, sorrow and regret as certain as sunrise and sunset. Misunderstandings and miscommunications, questions never asked and words never spoken, as predictable as the seasons.

Still, the stories my father needed to tell—and the ones I apparently needed to hear—did not *feel* archetypal to me. Why would they have? Lives unfold inside bodies that expire, but stories are retold outside those bodies, and have no time constraints, no end. As well, decades of halting conversations between us had made one thing clear: he'd never ceased thinking about those four names and narratives either. They were his sunrise and sunset, his winter spring summer fall.

He just didn't care to talk much about it.

Now he did care to talk. During another hospital visit that first winter, my father greeted my arrival with no fewer than four curt, prismatic utterances—as though he had been a passenger in my car, counting off the barns. He sat upright in the bed, headphones around his neck, intravenous drip and monitor positioned on either flank, like the bodyguards of a military leader whose enemies are vengeful. I was still fumbling with the gown and gloves that visitors had to don in the isolation ward.

My father said: "My mother was a drunk. My father didn't love me or my sister, Barb. For sure, not me."

And this: "My parents never came to anything Barb or I did. Not a school celebration. Not a parent-teacher meeting. They didn't care about us. Maybe that's why I never got involved in anything with you kids."

And this: "I don't have friends. Never have. Don't like people very much. You can't trust them."

And this: "Not sure why I'm still here. Don't see the point of it. Staying around for your mother, I guess."

I answered each remark with a bland "okay," mentally assigning them their excavation sites. Though they didn't quite align to the barns in my mind, it was a promising start. Sliding into the chair beside his bed, I was once again proximate to his right forearm, the freckles irradiated by hospital lighting. This also seemed fortuitous. While at least one of his comments made no sense—my father had attended hundreds of my hockey practices and games all those decades ago, driving us long distances at odd hours—I was distracted by the freckles, and then by what he said next.

"I dreamed about my dad last night."

"Really?"

"Charlie Foran. The Colonel," he said.

I had my grandfather's name.

"I never dream about him," my father continued. "Never think about him that much. Why would I?"

"Because he was your dad?"

"He was a bastard."

"But you dreamed about him . . . ? Was he in Ottawa? Was it during the war?"

"It was here."

My puzzlement must have showed.

"He was right there, standing at the foot of the bed," he explained. He indicated the spot.

"Had you seen him before?"

"In the hospital?"

"In your dreams."

"Almost never. Didn't want to see him last night either. In his uniform, hat on his head. Know what he said?"

"He spoke?"

"Pay attention," my father said. "I thought this stuff interested you."

"Sorry."

"'Wake up! Wake up! Don't sleep so much!'"

"I was just distracted," I said.

"Not you. Him. My dad."

"He said that?"

"'Wake up! Wake up! Don't sleep so much!' Clear as the hospital intercom when there's a real emergency. Someone checking out, most likely," he said with grim satisfaction.

"Charlie Foran, the Colonel, was there, at the foot of the bed . . ."

"And now you're here beside the bed," he said. "Staring at my arm, for some reason."

I kept my expression neutral, but secretly, I was thrilled.

5

David Bierk was a painter. He produced thousands of pieces over four decades. A few were as large as billboards, others as small as paperback books. His canvases could be epic, public engagements with art history and the environment, or private landscapes he alone could stake with his brush. That was his practice. How David lived his life varied less in scale. His thinking was only big, his plans only bigger. Appetites, ambitions, capacities, including for friendship, were uniformly supersized, and when an idea, a project, a person, excited him, he began the adventure by opening his arms wide for a hug. David fathered eight children with three women, the four youngest, all boys, with the love of his life, Liz. He was six foot three and had an athlete's physical grace. He also had velvet-blue eyes amplified by glasses, a warm, welcoming smile, a booming voice. An inveterate whistler and singer of pop songs, especially while he painted, he rarely stayed on key for long. Hard to fathom how Liz, who managed their business from the same studio, abided it.

I adored David. He spent every day and, I suspect, every night in a dialogue with the BIG world. He was determined to tap into its energies for his art. But he wished as much to serve as spokesperson for the universe's countless delights, freely available—if you knew to harness them. Between him and pretty much everything, it was love at first sight.

Diagnosed with leukemia in his forties, David was given a decade to keep on being his big loving, thinking, painting self. He was fifty-five when we first met. At the outset, I had trouble reconciling the news of his medical status with the man I was getting to know. Not the fact of leukemia at an advanced stage; rather, his response to it. He had two upcoming gallery shows and several more booked for the years ahead, was working with Liz on three different catalog projects, and had accepted multiple commissions, including one for an eighteen-foot-high piece to be installed in a hotel. He had those four sons, aged between ten and fourteen, as well as the older children, a studio to maintain and a rambling house to fix up, a private art collection, a dog and two cats, plus the car he drove for considerable distances without, it sometimes felt, once compressing the brake pedal. He and I played basketball at the local YMCA, and I had to negotiate his low post moves and sharp elbows. He hated losing at one-on-one.

Around this time, David and Liz were also moving studios. They had bought and were renovating an abandoned department store on the main street in our town, investing most of their savings. After a full year of construction, with the usual complications and cost overruns, they had renovated four floors, the main studio occupying the second. It ran a hundred feet deep by forty across and featured restored hardwood and an industrial ceiling. Light poured through arched windows at the front and angled through a two-storey glass wall at the rear, flooding a loading dock and storage area downstairs.

David's paintings, especially the epic canvases, looked good in the studio, as did the art of his friends. Furniture, plants, dogs looked good there too. Above all, people *felt* good in the new Bierk Art, lifted up and out of our daily routines, our grinding habits of thought. The studio—off the ground, but not too high—put any who visited it into a different frame. Life was being lived large in this generous space.

I visited David one afternoon in spring 1999. He had a typical project under way: to paint fifty landscapes onto eight-by-eight-inch copper plates, each for use as a slipcover on a book. The work of a month for another artist, he was hustling to finish the plates in time to drive into the city for an evening event. An assistant had adhered the copper plates to a board, allowing him to move from image to image with his brush, judging one against another, column by column, row by row. Even so, the task seemed gargantuan and impossible to achieve in the few hours he had allotted to it.

David did not agree. He painted with confidence, one brush dancing in his right hand, another often clenched between his teeth, paints squeezed out in dollops onto a palette. He was reproducing the same image, it was true, each plate just different enough from the other. But what allowed him to work so fluently was the landscape itself. He had been painting it for years, almost as a daily practice, the way others did yoga or said prayers. I had admired samples in the studio and in books dating back nearly a decade, although the scene had evolved, especially the intensity of colors and density of paint.

Today I was watching him reproduce the landscape another fifty times. A thought occurred to me: How come I had never noticed a source sketch or photo, a sample from another artist, near his easel? When I asked, David admitted such an image did not exist. I then wondered if the setting had been primordial to his childhood, or was a spot he slipped away to now, for secret inspiration. He corrected me there as well. He had never been to the place he depicted, nor laid eyes on it. He had simply painted it again and again, starting sometime in his forties.

These canvases—or copper plates, metal chads, slabs of concrete: his materials could vary—always divide into three tiers. Along the bottom is land, low-lying and scrubby, a river running through it, or maybe a pond. Rarely does the earth take up even a quarter of the frame, and it is recessed and placid, devoid of living creatures. In the busy middle tier are clouds, usually travelling, a canopy over anyone or anything on the ground. On top of this sky, however, above the clouds and invisible to the earthbound, is still another layer. Usually a full half of the painting, this highest space has no roof, and is radically different: vaulting, churning, suffused at once with light and dark, like depictions of a solar system being born. Near the center is often a gyre of paint, emerging below and stretching upward, as a flame does.

I recognized the uppermost sky. It was the firmament, the celestial sphere. The ancient Greeks called it the empyrean—the realm of pure fire. And my friend, by then in the tenth year of a ten-year death sentence, was painting it ever more urgently, applying cadmium orange and yellow ochre, raw sienna and burnt umber, while chatting with his younger, healthier friend about sports and art.

That day I did not think to ask: *Do you understand what you are painting?*

Nor: *Is it helping?*

Not even this: *What are you expecting to find up there in the pure fire?*

Later that same year—New Year's Eve, to be exact—Liz and David hosted a dinner in the studio. Liz fashioned a long, rect-angular table for guests near the glass wall and laid out a white tablecloth covered with candles and spruce sprigs, star-shaped mobiles hanging from the ceiling. On either side of the table were David's appropriation pieces, samplings of Rembrandt self-portraits, Donatello bankers, nudes by Ingres, flowers by Manet and van Dael. The art, the flickering candles, the snow-fall visible through the glass, lifted Bierk Art higher off the ground than usual. This was the perfect place to await the anx-ious pivot into a new millennium, assuage fears of pending grid collapse and civilizational reboot. Surrounded by friend-ship and love, nothing bad could happen to any of us.

David was not a drinker. He turned quickly tipsy when he did drink, like a comedian dropping into a character and staying in the part long past earning the laugh. His sodden self, garrulous and unpredictable, ruled until Liz ordered him to bed. Toward midnight, I found him on a couch with our eldest daughter, in conversation about the century soon to be launched, possibly with catastrophe. Nine-year-old Anna nodded wordlessly and bit her lip, her eyes widening at both the fervor of David's vision and the glass of red wine in his hand.

He could not believe how amazing her life was going to be. Her life, and the lives of all the kids in the studio. So much was going on right now in art, in technology, in medicine. Everyone was destined to be healthier and happier, more fulfilled. In the new millennium Anna and her sister, his children, young people everywhere, would be able to live as they wished, do as they wished, become who they are. There was no stopping the incredible stuff coming their direction—and had he mentioned the medical advances, soon to extend lives? Deep in his bones, David knew all this to be true. The future was going to be big; he was so glad for Anna and her generation; he was so grateful.

Liz joined us. She listened to her husband for a minute, then ordered him to stop spilling wine on a child. She and I exchanged glances, but I could not be sure we had communicated. *Has there been news about the leukemia?* I tried to ask.

Early the next morning, on January 1, 2000, my wife and I walked the six blocks home with our daughters. It was equally lovely outside the studio as it had been inside, hushed from

the snow and a winter storm, its own kind of drifting, sus-
pended time. The snowfall continued, a natural, non-scary
occurrence, and we declared ourselves and the friends we
cherished lucky to be alive in the so-far stable new century.
Along the way I began a mental dialogue with David, one that
I would continue for years after his death in 2002. I arc back
to it more and more of late, if only to hear his voice again.

Why do people sing, David?

Because we are ecstatic.

Why do we love love-songs especially?

Because they are B-I-G.

Why do we never stop singing?

Because we are going to die.

6

You have been puzzling out this riddle since you were a teenager and almost stepped off a cliff.

Lao-Tzu falls asleep by a stream. He dreams he is a butterfly fluttering through the air. In the dream there is no Lao-Tzu. There is only a butterfly registering the sunlight and breeze, sensing an animal on the ground nearby. Then he awakens. Now he is an animal by a stream, one who answers to the name his parents gave him. He notices a butterfly over the water, light glinting off its wings. Still drowsy, Lao-Tzu asks: Am I a man who dreamed he was a butterfly, or am I a butterfly dreaming he is a man?

A child gazing at the sky as birds dart by might pose this question, her sense of self easy and new, not yet a skull prison. Or an old person, relieved the prison door will soon fly off, pausing before a field of sedge grasses so towering that he sees no beginning or end to it. Or a wise human of any age standing at a riverbank and thinking: This isn't the same river I stepped in yesterday. It won't be the same river tomorrow.

Or a butterfly admiring its reflection in the water and thinking: Whoa, a human face?

You were nineteen when you first heard of Lao-Tzu. Now you are fifty-six. Why the near-lifelong puzzlement over the distinction between a man dreaming he is a butterfly and a butterfly dreaming he is a man? Because the parable has never quite *not* been on your mind, in your thoughts. In your body too, where you've felt it in constant play. The seam between awake and asleep, self and non-self, being you and being-something-else, keeps opening. What lies beyond? Who waits on the far side? Before you became a parent, you were reckless about the attraction to the seam, ready to throw away your one life. Now you are possibly more obsessed, but also watchful and humble. No need to step toward it; the seam will open soon enough, and take you in. Then you will be . . . what, the butterfly? Or the man? Truth be told, the parable still isn't clear to you—not yet.

You are a young adult skating on a river at twilight. The ice is glass and the snow a cascade. Air catches in your lungs. Though you laced up with friends at a cottage some miles ago, you are alone now, no voices intruding on the silence, no blade marks except your own. Walls of pine along either bank clarify the path. Heaven above drains to black. You speed up, strides strong and arms swinging in tandem, breathing ghost funnels. Faster, faster you skate, never mind the occasional rough patch underfoot or the curtain in the far extremity of your sight. No point glancing over your shoulder or slowing down. And gradually that curtain, which must be translucent, begins to pull back. Ahead lies more wind-cleared ice, miles of it, yearning

for a moon to illuminate its perfection. Not so far off is a bend
in the river.

Feel that?

You are an older adult visiting a cathedral. Locals, mostly
elderly, kneel in pews. A priest exits the confessional, head
bowed. Unimpressed, you glide past the altars and side cha-
pels and many statues of many saints, making for the exit.
Halfway down the transept, the marble floor starts to trem-
ble, as if from a tremor, early warning of a quake. A sonic
wash follows, no less physical, and by the time you have
sourced the drone—the choir loft above the west door, the
organ pipes against the wall, the organ near the railing—a
melody is rolling through the cathedral. Bach, you think, or
son or grandson of Bach, played on that organ, the musician
invisible from below.

Resolving to put a face to the music, claim it as routine—
if beautiful and eerily perfect—human activity, you unhook
a rope barrier and climb a winding staircase. From sixty
feet above, the cathedral is much, much larger, its dome
awesome and improbable. Adjusting for vertigo, you cross
the loft to the organ pit, expecting to find a woman or man
poised over the keyboard, the cantata or fugue by Bach, or
son or grandson of Bach, flowing from fingertips back to
pipes, and then out again. But the organ is empty, and the
music is not emanating from here. It comes from all around,
including, if not especially, beyond the low railing. You find
this equal parts thrilling and perturbing: music of the sky,

the empyrean, trapped beneath a roof, like starlings who live for generations inside these buildings, unaware they are in exile. At the railing, you lean out into that awesome bounded space, then lean into it, thinking this and that, and then not thinking, lucky you, at all.

Feel that too?

You are a parent studying the faces of your sleeping daughters. They resemble their mother, for sure, but with clear traces of your sister in the younger, and their maternal grandmother in the older. If photos are to be trusted, one child has the winsome smile of your grandmother and the other the bright smile of your wife's grandmother, a woman known for her expressive features. You make this study of your children every few months, sneaking into their rooms on nights when moonlight leaks around the curtains, watching their eyelids twitch and their lips move, marveling at the changes, the dissolves. One year, you see your mother in the facial structure of the older, the next in the younger. The following year, the youngest is all your father, the elder a couple of her maternal aunts combined. And you—where do you appear and disappear, begin and end, in these creatures? Nowhere, you think. Everywhere, you think.

Feel that as well?

It is also a seam, the movement of blood and memory through bodies and time. It is a daguerreotype made in the 1850s of people who may or may not be your ancestors, and where you find, in the second row, third from the left, a man who is, to all intents, you. He is shorter and skinnier, and his upper lip is lost beneath a caterpillar mustache. Otherwise, he is you and you are him, and the butterfly is dreaming he is a man—or the other way around.

7

While in hospital my father groomed himself every morning. He did so in the bathroom or, if not up for the walk, in his bed. I watched him perform his ritual one day in early 2017, at the outset of another extended stay, this time after six happy months back home. First, he dry-shaved, carefully rubbing his cheeks and chin, and then re-scraped the still-bumpy surfaces, the skin blushing, one or two nicks leaking blood. Next, he combed the remaining hairs over his skull. This too was a contemplative act, done as if he knew exactly the look he wanted, and could see it, even without a mirror. Satisfied, he wet his fingers with saliva and glued down uncooperative strands— just like he might have six decades earlier inside his tent, alone in the bush for weeks on end.

"How do I look?" he asked.

"Like you've places to go and people to see," I said.

"Good."

The compliment was truthful, from the neck up. The rest of his body was broken, and not fixable through self-care. The ridiculous hospital gown betrayed his condition. His shoulders, chest, belly and thighs were on intermittent display, often without him being aware, and showed the scars, needle pricks, bruises and blemishes consistent with both bodily breakdown and a tire-iron beating in an alleyway. Behind him, around him, were those machines, now three in total, beeping and pumping and closely monitoring both their charge and any who approached the bed. I half expected the machines to block me in the doorway, biceps bulging. *Who the fuck are you?* And then, turning to my dad: *Do we trust this guy?*

His arms were especially dismaying. They were desiccated, the muscles withered, veins burrowed under skin to evade needle probes. Only around the saline drip patched into his right elbow had any hint of musculature returned, but that was from swelling, the skin jaundiced. The arms were otherwise mostly blue and black, especially the inner elbows. Seated next to him, my gaze kept straying to those bruises, former gateways into the archipelago of his freckles. No adventures filled my head today.

Following my eyes, he said: "They've given up drawing blood from up there. Can't find any veins." He pressed the elbow patch with his other hand, like a nurse. "The vampires are working on the backs of my hands now."

"Ouch," I said.

"You know I don't feel pain."

I did know that. He'd repeated it often enough over the years. Land a hammer on a finger, slice a thumb with a saw, and Dave Foran would deliver a deliberately high and whiny "oo-uu-cc-hh," followed by an equally melodramatic wince. If blood flowed, he would watch it seep from his body, playing with the wound until told by one of us to please stop, wrap it in gauze and go get stitches. Sometimes he did these things, but usually he did not. He just wasn't feeling it, he would say—not a thing.

"I sure feel pain," I said.

"I'm aware."

"Was your dad the same as you—didn't feel a thing? Like when his nose was blown off in the war?"

"You remember that story?"

"I remember him telling me. I remember sitting in his lap and gazing up at the nose the doctors had rebuilt. We were visiting him and Shirley at their farm—"

"You barely knew him. Her even less."

"I'm not saying I did," I said. "I'm just saying—"

"*I* barely knew my father," my father said. "He disappeared for most of my childhood."

This was not entirely true. His father had not "disappeared" for most of his childhood. He had fought in the Second World War, becoming one of the longest-serving Canadian soldiers overseas—seven years in total. My father was aware of this, obviously. Still, I said nothing. I didn't want to talk about Colonel Foran and the war. I wanted to talk about Charlie Foran and his second wife, Shirley Foran, whom I had indeed barely known. And yet I had news of Shirley, four decades after she'd been erased from our lives.

"You have his name," my dad said, jumping into the stream of my thoughts, "and nothing else. You don't look like my old man. You look like me, maybe, or like your mother—but not like him."

"Anna looks like Ruthie," I said.

"You didn't know my mom either."

"I remember her a little."

"She was tiny, a bird. A drunkard by twenty-one. Already had her kids by then too. She probably shouldn't have," he said.

"Drunk so much?"

"Had kids."

I pictured a hammer smashing a fingertip.

"Hey, I saw a photo of your grandfather for the first time the other day," I said.

"Where?"

"On Google. A Wikipedia entry."

He waited.

"The computer . . ." I said.

"My grandfather died in '45, the very end of the war."

"His full name was William Michael Foran," I said. "According to Wikipedia. My real first name, plus Mike's."

This was entirely true. My brother was born Michael, and my birth certificate read William Charles—doming three generations of our family. But from early on I was called only Charlie or Charles, in honor, it would seem, of the grandfather I had barely known and the parent my father had barely liked.

"I didn't see him much," my father said of *his* grandfather.

"Maybe Barb did? Because she was older?"

"Barb?"

"Your sister? My aunt."

He flinched, although not—of course—at another hammer blow. "I know who Barb is."

Two of his machines made noises, one a beep and the other a belch, a goon squad bristling at a threat to their boss. The machines weren't wrong. We were circling the ruins now—Charlie Foran, Ruthie Foran, Shirley Foran, Barb Norton—and I was pushing farther in. The imperious father. The fragile mother. The intruder second wife. The co-damaged sibling. I wanted to explore all four, at once. But mostly I needed to tell him the news about Shirley.

Not long before, my sister Debbie had learned of Shirley's death. My grandfather's second wife outlived her husband by forty-one years, never remarrying and spending her final days in the farmhouse she and my grandfather had called home—the same one we'd visited as children. Debbie had attended her funeral, one of seven mourners, counting the clergyman, and ended up helping to carry the casket. Among the other six were a couple who had been neighbors and were overseeing Shirley's estate. They'd mentioned photo albums still in her possession, many featuring our father as a child, and asked if we—our side of the family, the estranged, never-heard-from side—wanted them.

My sister and I had driven out to the farm to see about those photos. I'd not been there since I was thirteen. Approaching it again, I felt momentarily lost. Much of the property had been reclaimed by bush; the barn where Charlie Foran kept race-horses had burned down; and the in-ground swimming pool had crumbled, its concrete floor sprouting roots. The house showed similar desolation. Most rooms had been cleared of furniture, but not of dust, and the air was clotted with mold. Shirley had died in a small room, its curtains tattered and car-pet stained, the bed unmade after a month. Next to the bed was a ventilator, and on a side table were an ashtray and bottles of liquor. There was a TV with an antenna. There were framed photos of her and Charlie on the walls, elegant wife and dapper husband, happy and in love at the racetrack, in restaurants, on holiday. All were in black and white.

I couldn't stay past ten minutes. The loneliness and suffer-ing were palpable, a poison creeping along the floor. My sister felt the same, and we gathered the mildewed photo albums, which sought to crumble in our hands, and fled. During the drive back to the city, we were silent, except to wonder about our Aunt Barb, whom none of us had seen in years. Had she known of Shirley's death? Did she know that her only sibling, our dad, was in his twilight? Barb and my dad didn't talk either, and Debbie told me she had recently learned something dis-tressing about one of Barb's sons, who battled depression. She'd heard that Barb was ill too.

Our aunt and her grown children lived ninety minutes by car from Shirley Foran's farm, and three hours away from our parents' home. My sister and I both lived in between.

Now, at the hospital, I told my father about the visit, and the photo albums, watching his face for a reaction.

"Shirley never liked us," he finally said. "She didn't like kids."

He had expressed these sentiments before. But something in his words never rang quite right: he'd been seventeen when his father remarried, and Barb had been almost twenty. Hardly kids any longer.

"They seemed in love," I said.

He cut me a look. "How could you possibly know that?"

"The photos on the walls. And in the albums. And the fact that she never remarried and returned to the farm to end her days. End them badly," I said, cushioning the sentiment.

"My mother wasn't much of a mother. Probably not much of a wife either. Shirley was young and glamorous and liked the things my father did—horses, gambling, restaurants, traveling in style. Who could blame him?"

"You did."

My father's face hardened. "I'm pretty beat," he said. "So are you, I think."

"I'll bring the photos next visit."

"What photos?"

I waited.

"Okay. Do that," he said.

"They're incredible. So many of you as a boy in Ottawa. Lots with Barb as well."

"If you say."

I got up to leave. Another long ride back to the city, work the next morning.

"Kiddo, you really don't look too good," my father said.

"Thanks."

"I mean it."

He did. Just as I meant my "thanks" for his concern. We had never been able to speak directly about our feelings. We had no shared vocabulary or even understanding around why humans had to sometimes talk about their worries and vulnerabilities, the things that kept making them sad. That left us no choice but to repurpose rote words and familiar concepts to serve as awkward metaphors for what was constantly on our minds, in our dreams.

"No pain?" I said to him. "Honestly?"

"Never."

"Not even in those arms?"

He pushed at the bruises with his fingers. "Oo-uu-cc-hh," he said. "Don't I look like a junkie now."

I wanted to shout: *You* are *in pain! And have been since forever.*

But maybe I had it wrong. And shame on me: badgering a dying man to help *him* understand all the things he could do so little about?

Except that he could do something about his only sibling, our ailing Aunt Barb. There I could help, a little.

"Have you talked to Aunt Barb lately?" I said in the doorway.

"Why do you keep mentioning her?"

"She's your sister."

"We were never that close."

"And yet you look so much like her."

"So you keep saying."

"I just think it would be nice for you two to talk."

"Kiddo . . ." my father said again. He closed his eyes and I, taking the hint, took my leave.

8

Four years after David Bierk's death in 2002, my wife and I held a twentieth wedding celebration in his studio. Liz Bierk had kept the studio intact, David's easel in its spot and brushes in their jars, tubes of paints in allotted trays, and their four sons, emerging as artists in their own rights, worked there sometimes. But with no new paintings to sell and no David to persuade with his big ideas and bigger vision, the business was winding down. As well, Liz had taken ill the previous winter, a bout of cancer she initially beat, only to have it roar back in the spring. She rose from her sickbed to attend the party in early August, her hair mostly lost to chemo, and was her usual gracious self with the sixty friends and family who filled the space she had built off the ground with her late husband. David was there too, and not only in the art on the walls. We had wanted them present in any form, and for whatever length of time, they could manage. Liz lasted until near midnight. David stayed until the lights went out. I kept glimpsing him on the couch where he had spilled wine on our daughter at the turn of the millennium, an arm draped across its back, smile wide at the dancing and drinking. His voice boomed in my head: "Gratitude, Charlie. Gratitude."

Liz Bierk died that autumn. She was fifty-two. Bierk Art closed around the time we left the town where we had raised our girls.

Several guests at the party for our twentieth anniversary had been the Bierks' friends equally. Others were one degree of separation away. A little time before, some time between, and mostly in the time after the deaths of David and then Liz, we solidified a circle of close friends who, directly or indirectly, traced back to them. The process was organic: people meeting, liking each other, finding things in common, and in turn introducing others. Had we thought about it, we might have viewed the period that followed as a small miracle, friendship not being easy for most of us after a certain age. We might also have declared it the final act of generosity and optimism of two generous and optimistic people.

Innermost in this circle were four couples. Weekends, we gathered in houses and apartments for dinners and parties. Weekdays, we met in smaller configurations for drinks, to see a play or concert, watch football or hockey. We liked to cook and eat and drink, worry over our teenage children and aging parents, careers and vocations, fat mortgages and no pensions, dogs and cats, sports teams and geopolitics, along with the personal habits we suspected we might soon need to improve. In our late forties and early fifties, we still had plenty of game left in body and mind, and now had each other as fresh support and backing—to puff up or call bullshit, depending on the night.

One friendship adrenalized me. Like David, J was a painter, a gifted one, and I had first met him when he rented a space in Bierk Art, to work near his friend. He and his wife had attended the millennium party, were part of the circle that tried to assist the Bierk family around David's death, had danced at our anniversary celebration, and then done all they could during the fallout from Liz's rapid decline. J was intense in his friendships, passionate in his views, and felt each of these death blows at least as much as, if not a bit more than, the rest of us. He and I shared our love of David, and then our grief, and then our love of Liz, and then our grief again. Music bonded us as well, and sports, and "eating only what you kill," as he described the artist's life. We talked about sex and love and family and friendship, usually every day, before we started our writing or painting, and if our own fathers—as men, as Dads, as future *us*, further into the palimpsest—weren't always top of the list of things we needed to sort out, they were never off the list either. Shortly after Liz died, I worked with J on the text for one of his shows, a short piece about, indeed, his father, whom he had lost not so many years earlier.

Our small circle didn't last. The intimacy, the intensity, the easy good times didn't endure for as long as I would have liked. And it didn't last between me and J. Not exactly. Not as I'd hoped. The reasons were unexceptional. People moved away.

People who stayed had arguments. People had disputes about how to live and whose company to best keep, and in the process grew tired, heavy and unhealthy, and, although secretly feeling strangers to their former selves, deflected much of this anxiety outward, making excuses and putting up walls. People got sad.

Who doesn't become sad? And who doesn't go strange for periods? I get sad and I go strange, as if no longer quite recognizing the gaze in the mirror or the voice coming from my mouth. I am not a different person—none of us can change our eyes or ears—but I am older and riddled with complications of the most mundane variety. Also, I have survived more than sixty years, lucky me, and along the way have registered more than a few inner shifts, wobbles and upendings. Essence is essence, but the self never quite settles. Not with so much happening, should we be lucky enough to live a good long while.

It is natural, is it not, that we present ourselves to each other, including the most cherished people in our lives, differently some days? Natural too that we struggle at moments to keep company with others as easily as we once did. Often, I ponder who David and Liz Bierk would be now, had they outlasted their cancers. In his late seventies, still lanky but with a paunch, David would be working fewer hours in the studio, his voice booming and his humming a tuneless drone. In her mid-sixties, eyes yet summer-sky blue and skin teenage smooth, Liz's days would be filled arranging retrospective shows and private sales, the weddings of their sons. David, I imagine, might be a quieter man, tilting toward introspection in his thinking and late-career minimalism in his art. Liz may well have emerged as the family extrovert, disinclined to keep her thoughts to herself any longer or defer to her husband. How changed they might be all these years later. How very much the same.

I imagine a scene: I book a table for ten in a private room in a restaurant. There is food and wine, preselected and served family style. Name cards at each place ensure the four couples are seated neither beside nor directly across from each other. That way, they will not be able to make purposeful eye contact with their spouses, and may share difficult thoughts with the group, feelings they have long wished to express. At either end of the table are David and Liz. Their names are on the cards as well. They are equal presences, the way portraits by masters on museum walls are at least as luminous as the people admiring the faces.

Atop each plate at the table is a list of questions. There are just three, agreed upon in advance. Terms for the conversation have likewise been settled. We stick only to the subjects posed by the questions. We do not talk about the past. No one leaves until everyone agrees we are finished. The final word—in whatever form it may take—belongs to the Bierks.

THE LIST:

- Have we become sad lately, gone a bit strange, and not known how to explain it to ourselves, never mind to our dear friends?

- Are we aware that we have much less time ahead than behind?

- Do we want to die in or out of love with the world, and with those few creatures whose paths intersected our own, the way shoulders rub and knees touch, fingers accidentally meet, at a crowded dinner table?

As I see it—so clearly that I ache with longing—the Bierks wrap up the evening with music. David hums, badly. Liz, a fan of Leonard Cohen, sings. Friends, she paraphrases, try not to be frightened. We are so briefly here. In love, we come in. In love, let us go out as well.

9

Your office faces south from the top floor of a century building. Once a factory, the building has high semicircular windows opening onto the Toronto skyline, and a blinkered glimpse of the waterfront at the foot of Spadina Avenue. From the window you gaze out at the financial district and watch the CN tower, a syringe with a bubble of air—or drugs—near the tip, flicker red, blue, green and yellow after dark. A streetcar runs down the middle of Spadina, and the sky over the city is often spectacular, especially when weather moves across the lake. On two different occasions you have noticed the tower, shrouded behind tiers of unstable rain cloud, tilt and then sever into two, the colors bleeding into the vapors and smudging the night. Rub your eyes, close and then reopen them; the effect, narcotic and beautiful, stays.

But mostly you observe the neighborhood below, a burbling stream of vehicles and bikes in the lanes, and people on the sidewalks, including the corner where a grocery shop thrusts bins of vegetables and fruits to the curb, forcing everyone into the street. You also study the birds. Pigeons, hundreds of them lining up along the ledge of an apartment building in your direct sight, ready to take flight on some command. They perform air shows throughout the day, maybe a dozen between dawn and dusk, although you are unaware of any schedule. As a result, you wait, glancing up from your computer every so often and then cursing when you find the ledge empty and the sky outside the window suddenly filled.

Initially the birds move as a flock, swerving and looping in between buildings, executing climbs and dives. Then they divide into squadrons, weaving in and out of each other, never colliding, not a feather ruffled. If choreography, it is dazzling and bold. If design, it is beyond comprehension.

You invite staff into your office. "Look at the birds," you say. "How about the intricacy, the elegance! Doesn't it make you wonder?" Your colleagues do look, and they do wonder. For a few seconds, they may wonder about the pigeons. Then, judging from their glances, they wonder about their boss, who stands at the window for long periods, sketching the air with his hand. This is how, by the way, you sometimes imagine your own father stood at the window in *his* downtown office, forehead and belly pressed to the glass, acting—or simply thinking—strange.

The staff don't know the half of it. Usually, the pigeons remain within the frame of the window. But should a performance stray outside it, you become agitated. What if the birds have broken rank and lost communication, and are now scattered? Suppose the squadron, steered by bad leadership, has slammed into a brick wall? Palms moist, you await their reappearance, desperate for that design to win out.

The birds always do return, surging back into view in formation and capping the show with a vertical climb. They alight back onto the apartment ledge, one after another, flapping until a space opens. All then clear out to feed before the next summons.

Several of the pigeons dine in a small square a block south of your office. The square, hidden from the window by buildings, lies on your walk home. It is a grubby area: a cheap motel and some derelict shops, a statue of Sun Yat-sen. On the ground, the birds are not so elegant, especially when bread scraps and seeds are scattered across the pavement. In their frenzy, they brush the tops of scalps and tangle up in feet, cause children to scream.

Elderly women feed the pigeons most days. They share occupancy of the square. Practitioners of a meditation sect originating in the nation of Sun Yat-sen, these women spend their waking hours protesting the treatment of their sisters and brothers back home, holding poses for extended periods, expressions serene but knees, arms and backs in presumed agony. They do this in all weather and seasons, wearing puffy jackets and toques, waving their arms to keep blood circulating. Pedestrians rarely slow to admire their dedication or take a pamphlet. But they do scold the women for encouraging the pigeons. The sidewalk is crowded enough. Let the filthy creatures eat elsewhere.

Sometimes you think you should talk to the women about the birds. Though their view of the pigeons is more earthbound, these women see what you see; perhaps they also feel what you are feeling. They too may be worn out and heart-sore, humbled by all the things they can't change and keen to understand how those things connect.

Here is what you imagine saying to them. *You know and I know what is happening here. Those may not be the same pigeons feeding in the square or perched on the ledge as last year. Next year many of the birds will be different again. Constant are the flights themselves—bodies in motion, bodies in time. You know and I know about ourselves as well. We are here now, and the world needs us, to a point, doing whatever it is we do. It certainly calls us to experience, to participate, to sing the abiding beauty and mystery. But then we too go away and are replaced by others who are—and are not—just like us. Constant are our songs and stories, drawings and dances, the prayers we create to the gods we fashion out of weather and mountains and animals and trees. They don't disappear.*

But you don't say that to the women on the square. You don't say a thing, remain silent out of respect for the weight and the cold, the weight of the cold dead. Only those birds on the square care enough to respond to our shared entreaties. Twice, three times, a day we scatter our bread and sorrows before them. They answer us with cooing sounds of oh-oo-oor and oorh-oorh. But then they too flutter up into sky, doing who knows what and bound who knows where.

10

One Saturday in late October 2017, I drove to the hospital to see my father. I had intended to get there each of the three previous weekends, but work and travel had held me back. As well, I had recently learned distressing news about our extended family. The news had triggered a protracted rage in me, one I could neither source nor anticipate. It could surge through my veins at any given moment and, because of this unpredictable irritation, I sensed I might not be the best company for him. But my father was also just weeks, or perhaps just days, from the end, and the immediate family had been put back on notice by medical staff. Visit soon, they advised us. Stay longer. Say whatever words you must say.

The ride north from the city, in a downpour that muted the autumn colors, did not augur well. I drove fast over those country roads, spitting stones up into the wheel hubs and spilling coffee on my shirt, and roaring by the collapsed barns, now individually tagged with family case histories. All were up in flames as I called out the names I had assigned each conflagration eighteen months earlier. Charlie Foran! Ruthie Foran! Shirley Foran! Barb Norton! Had a rural traffic camera caught me, I might have been mistaken for a drunk driver. Or a driver who was high. Or, more accurately, one who was low.

My father, too, was sure low. He had been in and out of hospital since the summer. Ailments, complications, treatments and consequences were on a repeat cycle. The stents in his kidneys would fail again, and doctors would ask if he wanted—really wanted—to go through another operation. He would reply, no thanks, why would he do that, there was nothing left for him. To us, he would say, "Why won't they let me go?" Then he would agree to the operation. Afterward, doctors would offer their refrain: "One tough hombre, Dave Foran. A born fighter." To me, he would say, "I did it for your mother. She still wants me around."

That was his spirit talking, or his fear, given his conviction that nothing lay beyond the last gasp—the sigh of the bear in the bush killed by the man with the Winchester 44-40. His body was, if possible, less equivocal about its prospects: there weren't any. No comebacks, no partial recoveries, regardless of how many additional thugs—sorry, machines—surrounded his bed with each visit. The machines were exactly the excess muscle added during the final hours of the supreme leader, in order to block weepy confessions of mass graves or hasty succession plans with idiot offspring.

He looked like a fearful old man. His brief hair revivification had come and gone, and his freckles had faded once more to parchment, the contents unreadable by the most expert archeologist. His skin had soured to skim-milk pale with patches of yellow seeping through. Even his skull appeared diminished, the melanin spots widening and the skin pulling taut, as though the rictus of a final, likely unflattering expression was already in the works.

On my walk from the parking lot to the hospital, I vowed to talk only of my father's accomplishments, the duties he had fulfilled, the people who loved him. I would boost that spirit and ease those fears. My anger would stay within my veins and off my face. The news that had triggered it would remain either unspoken—his preferred outcome, I knew—or discussed calmly and without judgment. Lifelong shame, and its generational impact, would not be on the table—and might never be, I was coming to accept. It was too much for him. It might be too much for us.

At the same time, I was carrying photos from the albums my sister and I had salvaged from the house where Shirley Foran died. My father had taken a cursory look at the albums during a spell at home in the spring—I had watched intently as he turned the pages—lasting maybe ten minutes with the faded visual records of his childhood, among them the multiple snaps of his look-alike sister, our Aunt Barb. Then he had closed the album and told me he did not care to see the photos again. Period.

In my pocket, meanwhile, was an article I had published in a newspaper a year before, in conjunction with the job I was doing from the top floor of a building in downtown Toronto. I was thinking we could talk about the piece, the job, instead of family. Better, easier material—although we'd rarely talked about what I did for a living either.

Five minutes into the visit, I abandoned the plan. "I brought along a couple of those photos from the albums," I said, from the chair beside his bed. "You may have missed them the other time."

"I saw them," he said. "You watched me look."

I held the photos out. "Do you want to look again? There are some sweet ones of you and Barb. Also, the photo of your mom and dad walking down the street. He's in his uniform and she's wearing mink. What city is that, by the way?"

My father's right hand, resting on his belly, did not move. Nor did he turn to me. He stared ahead, his other arm clinging to the pulley over the bed, a passenger on a crowded bus avoiding eye contact with strangers. The photos hung in the space between us until I withdrew them.

"You don't remember your grandmother, do you?" he said.

"I remember our last visit to her apartment."

"Exactly."

"Exactly what?"

"What do you remember?"

I repeated the story, which was more my sister's memory than mine. We'd rarely seen our Grandma Ruthie during her final years. But when I was twelve, our family had piled into the car to visit her in a tiny apartment in the city's west end. We found her in a strange state, stiff to our hugs, her body protruding bones and cigarette stink, the clingy stench of sherry or port. Her underwater eyes could not hold anyone's gaze; words slurred from her mouth, making no connection either. After she fell from her chair to the floor, my father said, "That's it," and ushered us back to the car. No explanation. No good-bye. We waited a half hour for him to reappear.

"What she said to Debbie?" my father said. "Want me to remind you?"

I shook my head.

"She asked her if she was my whore," he persisted. "My fifteen-year-old daughter. *Her* granddaughter. 'Are you his whore?' she said."

"She had a disease."

"Anna doesn't look like her," he said, refuting what I had observed of my oldest daughter. "I know you said that once. Not one bit, okay?"

"Sure."

"I don't know where you got that idea."

I attempted a final defense of my grandmother. "Maybe some people don't know how to live," I said.

He shot me a glance, hoping to summon the old Dave Foran stare. But with no blue left, there was no burn, no velocity.

"I've been thinking about this lately," I said. "How some people never seem to acquire the basics. To do right by their own. To protect those dearest. Nurture them," I added, studying his profile. "Love them, even if . . . they can't love themselves."

"Maybe no one taught them," my father said under his breath.

I asked him to repeat the remark.

"I said, maybe no one teaches you. My parents never taught me a single good thing."

I should have paused there. But I did not. "When I saw—when Debbie and I saw—how Shirley ended her days . . ." I said.

He bristled at the name. "Shirley? I thought we were talking about my mother."

"Maybe we're talking about both . . . I don't know."

"Forget Shirley. Ruthie never loved me or my sister, her own children," he said. "Plain and simple. Should I care if she loved herself any less?"

"Did *you* love Barb?"

He shifted in the bed, staring ahead. Had his body allowed, he would have got up and walked out the door. But I had him cornered.

"Barb is dead, eh?" I said.

Silence.

"Your sister . . ." I finally delivered the family news that had sent me into that rage. "She died a few weeks ago."

"Guess so."

"And no one thought to call you and Mom?"

"Guess so."

"Was there a funeral?"

"Don't know."

"Was she cremated?"

"We didn't talk very often."

"Not for four years, right?"

"We weren't that close."

"So you didn't know she had Alzheimer's the final two years?"

"She didn't call me either."

Why was I doing this? There was no point; it was cruel. "We could have gone as a family," I said anyway.

"Gone where?"

"To pay our respects . . . To Aunt Barb."

He waited, still clinging to the pulley, a stranger on a bus. "Her boy . . ." he finally said.

"I heard about that," I said. One of Barb's sons, my cousin, a quiet man who ended up living with his widowed mother, had taken his own life some while ago.

"He was always so blue," my father said. "There was something not right with him . . . Family curse, I guess."

"Depression?"

He shrugged.

"Like your mom?"

"No idea."

"On learning about Barb's death," I said, "I felt, I don't know, devastated."

Finally, my father fought back. "That's pretty dramatic."

"On fire," I added.

"What's it even got to do with you?"

"What?"

"My sister . . . what's it even got to do with you?"

He was furious now, the pulley rattling. Too late, I realized

the cowardice of my behavior. The machines, beeping and ping-
ing, should have escorted me out twenty minutes ago. Thrown
me to the floor in the hallway, boots kicking my ribs and head.

"You're right," I said. "Sorry. I have to go. Long ride back."

In the doorway, near the foot of his bed, my father gave
me a look that *was* devastating. I supplied the expression
with meaning: *This is just how it is. How fucked up people are.*

I gripped the door handle, scrambled for something kinder
to say.

He did the same. "I dreamed about my old man last night,"
he said. "Figured you'd want to know."

"Again?"

"What do you mean, *again?*"

"'Wake up! Wake up! Don't sleep so much!'" I said, quoting
the earlier dream. A dream, it was now clear, he had forgotten—
both having dreamed it, and having shared it with his needy,
greedy eldest son. I moved on quickly. "What did your dad say?"

"Not a thing. I did all the talking. But I couldn't hear any
words coming out of my mouth. We were walking along a
street. He was in uniform."

"Were you in the war with him?"

"I was a boy during the war. How could I—?"

"In the dream."

"It was Ottawa. I was a kid, maybe ten. He was there, not
sure why. I saw him."

I thought of the photo in my pocket of his parents walking
along a street together.

"What else?" I said.

"Nothing else."

I nodded, then told him I loved him, as I had been doing at the conclusion of each visit. He told me he loved me too.

"One more thing," he said, as I turned to go.

I waited.

"You really don't look great," my father said. "Something going on?"

I'd had no intention of sharing this, but now the words slipped out. "I have an appointment with a cardiologist."

"You do? Why?"

"A precaution."

"Losing some weight might help."

"Is that the one more thing you wanted to tell me?"

"Listen," he said, waving me back to his side. I stood beside the bed again, my hand out. "I'm not going into the ground, all right? Into the flames, please and thanks. Your mother knows it. Don't let her forget."

"Okay."

"Never visited my own parents' graves, not once. Why would you kids bother with mine?"

A dozen objections, arguments and scolds came to mind. "Sure," I said.

"And she wants a church funeral with a mass and one of those celebrations of life afterward."

I nodded.

"Don't let her."

"No?"

"No one will come."

"Of course they will."

"You think I don't know?" my father said.

I think you don't know, I said to myself. But I took his hand and held it, freckles on freckles, for a minute, maybe longer. His eyes welled. So did mine.

This was hard for us both, two shy, self-conscious men, not so comfortable in our bodies. With one difference: besides an eternal fascination, the son found unceasing change and unexpected possibility in human affairs; the father, only broken things that couldn't be fixed and people who couldn't be forced to love you.

II

Recently I tried explaining a change within myself to a friend. Starting a few years ago, I began registering strangers with an intensity that felt new to my nature. Like many, I had people-watched all my life, sometimes because of their beauty, sometimes because of an interesting countenance or expression. I had done so reflexively, and assumed others, including those subjects, were doing the same of me, for the same reasons. It was, I always supposed, about bodies: animals with similar gazes, appetites and predilections, sharing tight spaces, and being only too aware. No insult was intended by the watching, and none, I hoped, was given.

On the subway, a middle-aged woman resting her cheek against a pole, eyes shut and features hollow. In the park, an older man on a bench, staring at nothing while his lips move to a song on the radio in his lap. In the café, a young man, earbuds in, checking the mirror behind the counter, and the face of the barista, to see if he is making an impression. On the bus, the teenage girl curious about the boy across the aisle, her eyeballs like balloons on strings, floating up and then pulled down, over her iPhone.

At some point, however, this stopped being enough. I began to want to apply stories to these people. Where were they from and what had shaped them? How had they gotten from there to here, then to now? I wanted to know the dilemmas they were pondering, as we are all pondering dilemmas, all the time. I found I did not need to watch strangers for a longer period to widen my engagement. A snapshot—on that bus and subway, in that café and park—remained enough. After that, I could close my eyes and let the stories take shape.

But the fleeting presence of others behind my eyes wasn't the change I was attempting to explain to my friend. Not exactly. "These last couple of years," I said to her, "I've been closer to tears, or actually shed them, than at any time in the previous four decades. Since I was a kid, really, strapped at school by teachers or spanked by my dad. The stuff that causes my eyes to well up . . ." I added. "You won't believe it."

"Try me," she said.

"Those Falun Gong ladies who protest in a square on Spadina Avenue. What they're doing is hard and they're very sincere about it. Yet people pay them no attention. If anything, they seem annoyed by their presence. Except for the pigeons," I added uneasily. "And who knows where they go, once they fly away."

"Pigeons?" my friend said.

I thought of a better example. "A homeless man defecating in the laneway behind our apartment one night. Our headlights pinned him, and his face collapsed in shame. I recognized the guy. He sleeps sometimes in the lobby of the building where I work, or in the park behind the art gallery. We'd talked a few times, including one conversation where he monologued for fifteen minutes about notions of the self in eastern philosophies. He was so obviously intelligent, and so messed up."

"What else?"

"Pretty much every frame of the movie *Little Women*," I said. "The version with Winona Ryder and Susan Sarandon. We watched it twice a year as a family, and I used to squirm while the females around me sobbed. Now *I* pool up at the opening credits and never quite dry out. The look on Beth's face when she realizes she's caught scarlet fever from the German family she's been helping? Poor, sweet Beth. She doesn't live to see Jo and the professor get together, you know."

"Stop," my friend said.

"Or YouTube videos," I said, forgetting myself. "Especially of animals from different species befriending each other. So touching, and a reminder of the great, wider planet unrelated to the narcissism and violence of our species. Dogs hanging out with cows. Cats licking the feathers of wounded birds. There's one video of a rabbit—"

"Stop."

I drew a breath. "It's like I've shed a layer of skin. And I'm always cold. The weather these days . . ."

"Empaths," she said.

"Sorry?"

My friend repeated the word. It was new to me. A quick Google search defined an "empath" as someone having a paranormal ability to apprehend the emotional state of another person. I was puzzling over "paranormal" when she snatched the phone from my hand.

"Empaths," she said, not reading from a suspect website, "are nearly always the products of codependent households. As children, they take on the feelings of unhappy loved ones, usually their parents, and grow up believing they could and should fix their problems, or even be the solutions. As adults, they continue to feel responsible for the feelings of everyone they know, and of people they don't know. It leaves them a perpetual mess, slobbery and weepy and prone to listening to the worst pop music. Also, to liking cat videos," she added. "And a big, exasperated 'Wow' to that overshare."

"Maybe I'm just falling apart."

"Is that the same as changing?"

"I don't see why not," I said. I paused, thought better of saying something, and then went ahead anyhow. "It's probably about my father. Did I mention that he's very ill and it won't be long now?"

"Wow," she said again.

Here is a scene. You are with your family in a country hotel by the sea. Hard rains and lashing winds, fog creeping along bluffs visible through the window, have kept you indoors for twenty-four hours. Exasperated, you finally announce a hike, and wait to see who will join. Only your eldest daughter enlists. She is ten, small for her age but precocious, burbling with language and imagination. Secretly—or not so secretly—you are amazed by her, consider her closest to you in temperament, how she moves through the world. You are glad for her companionship.

At the door your wife, readying cups of tea to watch a movie with your younger child, says: "Be careful. Things turn wonky in places like this. You take a step you can't take back. You find the ground no longer under your feet." She asks you to send a text every half hour and extracts a promise from your hiking companion—the sensible one, apparently—that you will turn around, should the wonkiness become evident. "If there aren't sheep grazing on a slope," she advises, "don't go down it."

"Ooh," you say. "A prophecy."

"What's a prophecy?" your daughter asks.

The path you take overlooks the ocean. Views are obscure, even of cliffs thirty feet away, and the sea, widening to a vanishing point on clear days, is all felt sensation—roar and rumble, the carve of rock by water. After a mile of muddy trekking, you both are experiencing bliss. Or, you are experiencing it, and presume your child, like you in so many aspects, is also absorbing the wonder. You are both out in the elemental, "the force that through the green fuse drives the flower." Welcome green age! The poetry of Dylan Thomas comes naturally to mind in wild landscapes.

You hold your daughter's hand, except where the track narrows, and register her icy skin. Two things occur just as you are about to suggest heading back. After cresting a hill, the path drops into a gully. The gully appears to taper into ocean, a haze of cloud trails and spray. That can't be right. There must be an in-between zone; earth and sky can't simply co-join. Wiping your eyes—the poncho hood is useless against the rain—you judge the severity of the slope, the funneling track and glimpse of raging sea, and think: *Wonky*.

"Beware the sheep!" your daughter says.

Three sheep graze a third of the way down, coats filthy and red dots on their rumps. Reassured, you watch without objection as the girl veers onto the grass. She slips immediately, regains her footing and adjusts her stance, stepping sideways, one hand supported by the earth. "Sheep, sheep, sheep," you hear her count.

"Careful," you say—or think to say.

At that moment, your phone vibrates. It rings too, but the wind swallows the sound. Fumbling to position the phone, you raise your other hand to protect the screen. ". . . getting worse . . ." your wife is shouting. "Can't see the path from the window . . . come back now."

And you are invaded by a thought. Why does she seem so distant? As if her voice lives only in your head and heart, your memory of timbre and tone, touch and taste. For you are separated by the seas, a sailor into the third year of a voyage to the antipodes, with scant certainty you will ever return to your village, your cottage and hearth, the bed upstairs and the woman in it; the one soon to weep at the news, by then many months old, that your ship went down somewhere near Van Diemen's Land.

The strange reverie is shattered. Your daughter screams once, her voice high and sharp. Barely three seconds have gone by, yet everything has changed. She is no longer on her feet below the trail. She is on her backside, a toboggan descending an icy hill. How severe is the gradient? How slick is the ground cover? Much more than you first thought. Even sturdy-footed sheep must find the gully treacherous.

But you see no sheep. There are no sheep here. With reason: this ground is wonky; it is lethal. There is only your child, hurtling toward the precipice, the drop into the ocean below.

"Hold on," you shout. "I'm coming."

What choice have you? Velocity is going to win out. The

fuse will drive the green flower. You can watch her disappear over the edge and then weave a path, clutching at heather and testing each step. You can drop to your knees and crawl to the rim, poke your head over. Maybe you find a ledge beneath, and her on it, terrified but safe. Tell yourself that. More likely, you see nothing, except the whole picture: sky, sea, spray, seabirds. But not your daughter. Never again.

Then you do what? Climb out of the gulley and shuffle back to the hotel with your tale of misery, your forever devastation?

Or you keep her company. Confirm your love, your commitment to, *haha*, protect. Declare that you and she are one being now, and that you feel no fear—and neither should she. Only gratitude for this moment together.

Also, you get to see her face again, and be absolved of your sins by the trust in her eyes.

Only as you push off do you remember the phone, still in your hand. You hope your wife hasn't been listening. You hope the signal was lost. Even so, you say with even less logic than your evocation of a sailor at sea: "I could court her vision in America." A line from a song about emigration and leaving your known love and life behind.

In no time you have caught up to your daughter and are clutching her to your chest. Your combined weight adds further velocity; fused together, you *are* some force, some fuse. Earth gives away and sky opens.

Over you both go.

———

Here is another scene. You are on an unplanned holiday in Thailand—your wife and two daughters, in a riverside hotel in Bangkok. It is April, the heat incinerating. The air, difficult to breathe out or in, gauzes the sky, like netting in a bird sanctuary. Sidewalks are pliant, and dogs collapse in streets, tongues out and sides heaving. Even a short walk with luggage leaves you clammy, forehead throbbing, needle pricks along the temples. Next comes a slow trepanation, using chisel and hammer, to release the sunstroke from your skull. For the following thirty-six hours you lie delirious in the hotel room, sipping water. Your family enjoy the pool and buffet restaurant.

Once recovered, you join them for cruises along the Chao Phraya. Up and down the river you travel, using public transit, long-tailed wooden boats that ride low and belch plumes of diesel. On a pontoon you all wait toward the end of one afternoon. A dog shares the dock. When a daughter pets it, the animal rises, tail wagging but rear legs lame.

"It's boiling," she says of its skull—as she has been saying of yours.

The girls go quiet as the dog drags itself to where two saffron-robed monks sit on a bench. Animal and humans trade smiles.

The water taxi approaches. A conductor uses a sequence of whistles to instruct the driver how to align the boat with the pontoon. Passengers must leap on board and be mindful that the gap can abruptly widen. You go first, to help the others, and then your eldest and your wife, cross over. But your younger child hesitates, her expression panicked. The conductor whistles and the stern drifts out.

"Take my hand," you say twice.

She finally steps across. "You almost left me behind!" she says from the deck.

"The monks would have looked after you," you answer. "And the dog."

The river races a few inches below the gunnels. Sun and moon eventually share the sky, and the temples along the banks are serene, the faces of children awakened by song. With nightfall comes a breeze, the taxi charting its route within a path of watery moonlight.

"When the moon is full, it means God is watching us," your younger daughter says. "When it's half-full, he's only half watching."

Later that evening, your wife, observing the girls eat plates of fruit at the hotel, whispers: "I bought travel insurance at the airport. I'm not sure why."

Into the second week of the holiday—you actually live in Hong Kong; it is month two of the SARS crisis there; schools are still closed, and social contact frowned upon, businesses shut down—you suggest a new setting. Instead of a beach, you sell them on the ancient capital of Ayutthaya, a short train journey to the north.

"Who wants to ride an elephant?" you say. "In a city so incredible outsiders once declared it the most beautiful place on earth?"

King U-Thong established his capital in 1350 on an island at the confluence of the Chao Phraya and several lesser rivers. Three centuries, five dynasties and thirty-three monarchs later, Ayutthaya had grand palaces and canals, spires called prangs and monuments known as chedis, row upon row of stone Buddhas and murals in jadeite and marble. Surrounding the sacred island was a trading town. Ships flew the ensigns of Japan, Holland, France and England. Silks, spices, sugar, tea and teak were bought and sold. Embassies opened. Merchants built grand homes. The Japanese had their own quarter, and the Dutch received royal permission to erect a cathedral, the Christian God being no threat to the Lord Buddha.

But the Burmese were a threat. They kept trying to sack the capital, and laid siege again in 1765, using cannonades and fireboats. The city held out for fourteen months. By the end, the remaining Imperial Guard did not expect any mercy to be shown. Townsfolk, though, may have had hopes. To no avail: invading soldiers slaughtered soldiers and residents alike, including all women and children. Though most soldiers sacked Ayutthaya on foot, swords bloody and eyes bulging, a lucky few oversaw the carnage atop battle elephants. Trained to rampage, these awesome creatures crushed anything in their path. Palaces, prangs, chedis, Buddhas and murals were first assaulted by elephants and then desecrated by men. Gold was stripped, jewels removed. Fires were lit.

And the destroyed city abandoned.

And the jungle moved in—forgetful green time.

You pile into a cab after lunch and cross a bridge onto the island. Ayutthaya is now a historical site, only the royal city recovered, if not exactly restored—bleached stone ruins spread across an open plain. The elephant enclosure also sits on the plain and has a roofed waiting area and a shrine to Ganesh. Six elephants await riders. The animals wear tattoos from a recent festival: red markings around their eyes and blue-and-pink vines over their trunks, leaf bracelets encircling their legs. Your girls choose a young female with tassels dangling off her ears. The driver helps them up to a wicker settee canopied by an umbrella.

Your daughters wave. "Bye, bye," they say, minor royals on colonial parade.

Your wife says, "We're not losing them. Not yet."

The ride is scheduled to last an hour. You announce a walk and invite her to join. She declines, citing the gagging heat and glaring sun, the zero shade, except in the waiting area. She asks if you will wear a hat. Your shrug triggers a warning. Once the girls are back, your wife advises, they will wait exactly fifteen minutes before getting a cab to the hotel.

"Stay out all night, if you want," she says. "With the cicadas and snakes, the hallucinations you want so badly to free from your leaky skull."

For a while you wander beneath the trepanning sun and among the ruins. Next, you lie in the partial shade of a giant Buddha hand, long ago detached from its body. Shirt soaked through, eyes closed to the lime sting of sweat, you succumb to a not-unhappy truth. Your head *has* split open, a hole that no hat would have kept sealed.

Ayutthaya is burning. Soldiers murder and destroy, their battle cries deranged. Elephants cry out as well, calls tremulous with rage and, possibly, dismay at what they are being forced to do. Everywhere things are in flames, on land and water. The air carries a stench.

Who is witnessing this? A coolie who loads the hulls of ships for meager pay. A man with a wife and two children, a bamboo hut easily put to fire. No assigned name. No place in remembered history. Heavy any father's heart, cognizant of what is about to befall his loved ones, his cherished known world. Heavy his mind, aware that he is small and useless, driven, for all his prayers, by his own deranged desires, his own unappeasable self.

Scramble down to the river and find a barge. Lay onto it the bodies of the woman you adored and the children you made— made of love and faith and a shy hope of speaking humbly to eternity through the flow of shared blood in veins—together. Then cast off. Hold them, tightly, lightly, your last breaths their first breaths now. Float as a family out into the Chao Phraya. Float down to the Gulf of Siam. Pray to the Lord of the Lotus. Pray to be, at long last, awakened.

One of these scenes is real, the other is not. Even now, you are never sure which is which.

PASSAGE

The look on my father's face that November afternoon.

For the second visit in a row, I arrived at the hospital with one agenda—to show only support and unconditional love—but followed another, less gracious or kind. I had the results from a stress test on my heart and wanted him to ask about it. I had the same newspaper article in my pocket, now a year old, and still hoped he would suggest I read it aloud to him, something we had never done before.

When he didn't ask about the test, I volunteered the good news.

"Dodged one, eh," he said. "But what about next time?" He tried the familiar joke, snapping his pajama bottoms to boast of his slimmer waist. But his hands shook, and his fingers could not grip the elastic.

"So, we're both doing okay," I said.

"Speak for yourself."

"I'm not."

"I bet," my father said. "Look at you."

That threw me. I pulled out the article. He asked what it was, and I offered to read it to him. "Maybe later," he said.

Here is a small part of what I had published: *It is important to speak frankly here. All of us are accidents of time and place. None of us did anything to deserve easier access to everyday dreams, and none of us can claim a superior genetic composition or a bigger, shinier heart.*

Now, the more I reread this paragraph, the harder I puzzled over why I had written it at all—the occasion, a piece on immigration and belonging, didn't quite align with the tone—and why I was desperate for my father to hear the words. Maybe I believed he could help me understand *my* heart and head?

I had often wondered what he thought of my work. Not so much the content of any book I published as, oddly enough, the form. Form mattered a great deal to me as a writer. Form was, I eventually came to realize, my body, as much as my mind, on the page. And where else had form emerged from, except my parents? My body *was* my parents, one generation later, and I was beginning to feel like all of us were on a barge, floating out into a river, down to a wider sea.

But my father had almost never asked about my writing. And he didn't now.

We didn't discuss much that visit. Not Charlie Foran. Not Ruthie Foran. Not Shirley Foran. Not Barb Norton. I was too tired and rueful to steer us back to these wounds. He was too frail or sad to pretend to be okay with my latest rude inquiries.

"Not even four o'clock," I finally said, "and it's dark out. I should get going."

"You have to?"

"I should."

That's when he gave a longer and clearer version of the look he had first shown me the previous month. This afternoon, I studied the expression. It conveyed a storm system of emotions: shock, terror, helplessness and surrender, along with the draining of any lingering hope. The expression belonged to a human looking in a mirror and seeing nothing, not even a shadow. It was also Janus-like. One face was of an eighty-five-year-old man astride the grave; the other, a ten-year-old boy on a crosstown walk. More precisely, it was the boy in the photos my sister and I had rescued from my grandfather's house. He looked frightened too, but not at the prospect of never seeing loved ones again, or of extinction. His expression suggested he had lately learned something crushing about adults, information that would change him forever.

The earth does not care that I am leaving it, old Janus lamented. *The earth will never be an easy place for me,* young Janus foretold.

Showing me those faces, sharing such feelings and fears, was my father's gift. He offered the gift twice, and twice I failed to recognize his generosity.

The second time, I was an hour into the drive back to the city, old Janus and young Janus both projected onto the front windshield—dualities, I supposed, although, viewed side by side, they seemed closer to a single entity in flux—when I realized my mistake. Pulling over in the dark, I pounded the steering wheel. I also debated turning around and forcing my way past the thugs into his room, and his good graces. Instead, I told myself I would make up for it the next weekend.

I used the interim to prepare a list of things I would say and swore on my shame to sit by his bed until I got through them. Not for a second did I delude myself that the list was for our mutual benefit. Confession and contrition are solitary, no matter if there is someone listening behind the screen.

Here was my list of things:

- Your courage these years, especially these last months. As if someone, not a surgeon, keeps cutting away pieces of your body while you lie strapped to the bed. "You okay with this?" the cutter asks. "We'll assume so." Where are they injecting needles into you now? How long does it take to fill vials of blood for further follow-up tests to the tests already done for the procedures previously tried and failed? Days you barely move, the urine bag bloated. Nights you mostly lie awake, thinking the same old thoughts, hammer and nail into a surface that will not be breached. Each visit I make to the hospital should open with one song of praise and end with another, proclaiming your courage, stoicism, and general good cheer under the most inexplicable of human burdens: the one that expects we should suffer and wait, suffer and wait, to get snuffed out.
- Your mother. My Grandma Ruthie. Can you please talk a little about her, beyond her problems? There must be

more to share: her as a girl, a young bride, a single mother with two kids. Those photos tell other tales from your childhood.

- Grandparents. I wish we'd had them. You and Mom were essential to Mary and me as parents, Anna and Claire as children. Grandparents really help.

- Your old friend Jimmy Picard, best man at your wedding. I loved Jimmy, his warmth and self-deprecation, the kindness in his eyes. I loved him like an uncle, certainly like family, and was confused when you two stopped being close. Did Jimmy turn strange on you, or you on him? That's been happening to me as well, and I could use advice. Good friends really help too.

- Dreams of our fathers. The other night I dreamed about you as a boy in Ottawa, making that epic walk across town to visit your uncle and aunt. The relations who were supposed to look after you and Barb while your dad was away at war. The aunt who answered the door and maybe set your features, and some of your character, for good. In my dream, it's your father, Colonel Foran, who opens the door. In his uniform, his pencil mustache and Brylcreem hair. "Wake up! Wake up!" Charlie Foran says to you—to us. "Don't sleep so much!"

- Parenting. One thing I know for certain: had we been hiking along bluffs in bad weather, and I tumbled down a gulley to a precipice, you'd have kept me— or my brother or sister—company. Eyes open. Full awareness of the consequences. You knew that much about love and protection, and you were brave.

- My waking dream of you and Aunt Barb. A frail old
  man, mobile with a walker, shuffles into the room of
  someone he has known all his remembered life. She is
  a frail old woman, hair white and eyes gray, expression
  vacant and smile nervous. He says: "I'm Dave and
  you're Barb. You don't recognize me any longer, I
  realize, but we look alike and walk, talk, tilt our heads
  alike, and I've a hunch we've a lot more than that in
  common. I'm not busy, you're not busy, and this life
  is so lovely and strange. Why don't we chat and see
  where the simple connection of my being here,
  and you being here, leads us. No recounting of any
  miserable history. No replaying of any family reel.
  Anyhow, what history, what reel? All gone now, sure
  as the names and dates on graves rubbed clean by
  weather. What do you say, Barb? Ready to talk to Dave?"
- My waking dream of you and Mom. An elderly couple
  sit before a high window, the curtains open. Light
  floods through the glass, forming a rectangle on the
  floor. Inside the room, the light is yellow-gold and
  soft; dawn or twilight, it's hard to tell. Outside,
  something bigger is happening. Palpable through
  the glass is radiance, unrelated to day or night, dark
  or light, beyond what any human can gaze upon
  or absorb through the skin. It shimmers. It hums.
  Neither comfort nor menace, the light contains a
  draw, a pull upward. Even the rectangle on the floor
  has a lifting energy. The couple dwell within this
  unstable frame. Any second, they might also get lifted.

Any second, they might burn up. Foreheads touching
and fingers entwined, they keep silent and still, not
wanting to trigger events. They close their eyes and
listen to each other's thoughts and non-thoughts—two
animals, breathing together. They could be siblings,
could be friends. Most likely they are happy wife and
husband of sixty-two years, reunited at the close of
day, and now sitting quietly, companionably, to see
what comes next.

That was my list, and my apology.

But when I reached the hospital, my father was asleep.
He lay on his side, face turned away from the visitor's chair,
encased in even more machines. I watched him, wandered the
hallways, dozed a night in a waiting room alongside my sister,
and then watched some more. When it became clear the sleeping could last for good—the nurses asked us not to wake him
up—I sat back in the chair and whispered into his ear.

You were a good father and husband.

You were a good man.

You should be proud of all you accomplished.

You should let the shame slip away.

You should slip away if you're ready. Slip into it.

The usual assurances and consolations. The things people
say to each other—or ought to if they are half-decent.

Thirty-six hours later, I got the call. Though I jumped into
the car and drove fast, I missed my father by twenty minutes.
His wife and daughter were bedside when he died, a grandson

and daughter-in-law down the hall. We took turns sitting with the corpse. Avoiding his face, which had indeed been caught in a pitiless rictus, not Dave Foran at all—not at age eighty-five or ten—I used our remaining moments together to make a final trip through the archipelago of his arms. Those freckles were still a map, one offering to be deciphered, if not followed. As a boy I had always started my journey at the elbow, steering south. Today I headed north from the wrist, saving the most difficult waters, the heaviest concentration of uncharted isles, for voyage's end. Once or twice my fingertip ran ashore in a cove, a false creek, and I had to backtrack and chart another passage. But I kept going, northward bound, not slowed by signs of seasonal onset, piercing wind and gathering ice—the forever winter, the lasting quiet.

Exactly what my father would have expected from his eldest boy, born just tough enough for this cold country.

PART
TWO

14

For a month after my father's death, I could hardly bear to think about him. I thought about my mother and my siblings, and I thought, naturally, about myself, especially how tired I felt, how bad I looked. But about him, almost nothing, as if he weren't gone or, stranger still, had never existed.

Twice during that month, I deliberately cut myself to see if it would hurt, if I would experience pain. This wasn't true self-harm—just a sliced fingertip, a scratch that bloodied my thigh. I was curious as to what I might feel, without being sure why, and then relieved that both cuts *did* hurt, and that I had no desire to wound myself further.

The problem was, I was meant to be writing my father's obituary for a newspaper. I had promised my family I would do this, and I was anxious to keep the promise. Still, I kept making excuses about my health (so-so), my job (demanding), the darkest days of winter (blues). Uncharacteristically, I provided the specifics of my ailments to any who asked: a torn-up knee and rheumatism in the hips, strained chest muscles, including a dull ache, like the waning throbs of a wasp sting, in the deep center. Too much caffeine and sugar. Too little sleep. An off-kilter gait I discovered only when I examined my boots and noticed that the right corners of both heels were ground down.

An old friend said, apropos of my boot anecdote, "Well, you do behave like a passenger in your own body."

"What?"

He elaborated. "Be careful about the other people in the car. You're not driving solo, you know." Again, I said, "What?" Then added: "I've had my license since I turned sixteen. I'm solid behind the wheel, thank you very much."

What I wanted to say to my friend was this: "How I feel right now is like one of those floppy inflatable Santas people put on front lawns—empty and ridiculous." But he would have asked why, and I would have had to reply: "No clue." Or I might have added: "I feel vulnerable like never before." But once more, he would have asked for details, alluded back to the passenger/driver metaphor. And my reply as to why I felt vulnerable—"No clue," also once more—would have ratcheted up the interrogation, which wasn't the desired outcome.

Finally, deadline looming, I forced myself to think about my father. A new question took form: How could I write about him without him being still *in* his body? True, the version of that body I'd observed most recently—decayed, diminished, under extreme duress—was hardly material for a celebration of life, unless conducted by Samuel Beckett. Imagining his face was no better: all I could summon in that first month was the after-death rictus, mouth gaping and teeth out, or else the old

Janus he'd shown from his hospital bed, a wordless howl. At least his ravaged body and agonized facial expressions had been real, a high brick wall of corporeal being that I hadn't been able to see above or beyond when he was in hospital, but which I'd still been able to walk right into, bruising a cheek and bloodying a nose, any time I wished. With that wall gone, my father had vanished, at least temporarily, and I could no longer conjure the man.

Or maybe I could, if I tried harder. But I did not yet care to admit to my head what my body already knew. I was adept at keeping mind and body separate—knowing, though not really; seeing, though only partially. My mind preferred to work alone. My body sulked at being left out of the conversation. My mind had no time for such nonsense. My body stewed over having its concerns rebuffed. One hated being expected to always factor in how head and neck, chest and stomach, muscles and joints "felt"; the other couldn't understand why feelings weren't thoughts, and vice versa, every moment simultaneously corporeal and cerebral in harmonious proportion.

Speaking for my mind—the favorite—I formulated an answer to my body's complaints about neglect. As a child, I had liked to sit near the tabernacle during mass. From there I'd had a clear view of the action. I could see God's mind slip down from heaven, via a shaft of light bathing the sanctuary, and slide into the tiny chamber where he temporarily dwelt alongside his son. On cue, the priest would open the tabernacle door and bring out God's only child to serve to worshippers during communion. As the priest always said upon distributing the wafers: "The body of Christ." (And we answered "Amen" and made the sign of the cross.) There was the son, a powdery wafer, and, on special occasions, there was his blood, a sip of wine. Every Sunday, the son got eaten; every Sunday, the father did not. Instead, his mind traveled up and down from the dome of dark blues and blacks, blinking stars and smears of constellations, that roofed the roof over the roof of the earth.

Mind or body: Which traveled further and lasted longer and even got to experience the enormity and mystery of that vaulting sky? *That's* who should be in charge. Or so I told my body.

Eventually I was able to write the celebration of my father's life. The allotted word count was five hundred, not much, and the format of the obituary involved selecting three descriptions of the deceased for the byline. Once I came up with active, positive words to describe my father—"woodworker, history buff, dancer," instead of, say, "neglected child, bear killer, solitary adult"—his outline began to reappear, minus the death mask and ravaged corpse. After that, I concentrated on telling a few good stories about him, and attending to the simple and obvious forces driving any human life: what we like to eat and drink, what we enjoy doing with our minds and bodies; what and whom we love.

> **David Foran:** *Woodworker. History buff. Dancer. Husband. Born July 6, 1932, in Ottawa; died Dec. 2, 2017, in Bobcaygeon, Ont.; of serious health issues, including kidney failure; aged 85.*

Dave Foran loved Hank Williams and Hank Snow, John Wayne and Gary Cooper. Red wine pleased him greatly, as did baked beans and extra-old cheddar cheese. He was passionate about history, especially Canadian and British, and would take his eldest son on drives around Ontario to point out the remaining Orange Lodges—the source, he believed, of much that was narrow-minded and grim about the province of his upbringing. He worked most contentedly with his hands and, for a while, built model chariots and crossbows that were put on display at the local library. Once retired, he crafted pine stools, mail-boxes and bird houses.

He loved the beauty and sensuality of cats, even more for their cold, killer hearts.

For sure, Dave Foran loved his three children and, by the end, five grandchildren and one great-grandchild. The grandparent role suited him especially well: helping his grandsons build a tree fort; watching teen movies over and over with his granddaughters.

Above all else, though, Dave Foran loved Muriel Foran, his wife of 62 years. They met in small-town Northern Ontario in the early 1950s. She was second youngest of 12 children born to a mill worker. Dave had survived a disastrous Ottawa childhood and gone into the bush, where he staked claims and hunted his food. Stories of that time and place suggested a reckless young man, the kind that often did not see his own 25th birthday, or else

ended up a rooming-house denizen, his best days long
behind.

But he got lucky. While convalescing in Blind River,
he met Muriel Fallu, a schoolteacher. Soon they were
married and living in a tiny house in town. Soon after
again, they were in the suburbs of Toronto. Children,
friendships, a career managing shopping malls, all followed. Happy, positive things—the opposite of that
childhood, or a protracted life in the bush.

His marriage helped him become a functioning husband, father and friend. He never lost that edge, however,
and once, in his late 60s, floored a man half his age for
insulting his daughter. He had come through a personal
fire, and Muriel was his salvation.

Dave and Muriel Foran loved to dance. To jive especially, the hip-hop of their courtship days. They jived fast
and fluid, at ease as partners, lovers and best friends.
Well into their 70s they danced with such joy, astonish-
ing their grown children, who looked away in deference,
sensing that the act was, ultimately, private.

In his own final years, Dave was mostly bedridden, if
still his mischievous, unfiltered self. Wife and husband
could no longer dance. But they were together, pretty
much every hour of every day, until the end, and Muriel
Foran, née Fallu, was never less than the great, sustaining
love of his life.

15

"Are you the boy who keeps using my name?"

This is how your grandfather greets you at the door to his house.

"You look like your mother," he adds.

"My mom is French," you say.

"And your old man is Ottawa Irish. Long line of Forans and McGradys and O'Neils. Your parents are Catholic with Catholic—a sensible match."

Your older sister, Debbie, almost eleven, kisses her grandfather on the cheek. She seems to know him better.

"Your sister is a dead ringer for Barb," Grandpa Charlie says to you.

"Who's Barb?"

He drags on a cigarette. He has silver hair and a pencil-black mustache and smells the same as your father does: Old Spice and Brylcreem, top shelf in the bathroom cupboard.

"She's my only daughter," he finally says. "Your only aunt."

About this, you are puzzled. You have ten aunts, called *tantes* in French, whose names you recite during the long drives to visit them: Marie, Helene, Lucille, Anna, Betty, Catherine,

Delisca, Rita, Pauline. Plus, Cecile, a nun living in Rome with the Pope. Then you remember the orange-haired woman who looks like your dad in a wig. "Oh yeah," you say. "Aunt Barb."

"That's her."

Your family are visiting Charlie and Shirley Foran on their farm outside the city. Unlike trips to your *tantes* and *oncles* and *cousins et cousines*, which are frequent and last for weeks, you can't remember the last time you saw the farm. It has a barn with horses and a pond with frogs and small fish. There is an in-ground pool for summer swims. The house is made of stone, with a curving staircase off the front hallway. On the walls are paintings of horses and photos of Colonel Foran in uniform, of him and Shirley in restaurants. On the tables in those photos are bottles and glasses and ashtrays laid out like cemeteries, some of the stones upright, others toppled.

In the family room you perch on the stool that your grandfather, seated in the armchair, uses for his feet. Your sister and mother are in the kitchen helping with lunch, and your dad has taken your five-year-old brother to see the barn. They went there right after Mike said, "Who's Shirley?" in front of her.

"Did your nose really get blown off during the war?" you ask, gazing up at your namesake.

"The bridge I was on got blown up. A plank ripped the nose right from my face."

"And broke your back too?"

"Your dad's been telling you all this?" he asks, like a kid in the schoolyard asking his friends if a girl *really* said she liked him.

"Just one time," you answer. Your father has probably told the story ten times, but you don't want your grandfather knowing it. You aren't sure why.

"That was a different accident. Blackout on the base, the air-raid sirens blaring. I'm crossing the tarmac in a Jeep. Can't see my hand in front of me. Can't hear myself think either. My batman, fellow by the name of George Smythe, a good guy, family man, he's driving, of course, and cuts the headlights, as per regulations. I glimpse a wall of black, and tell him as much—'Smythe,' I shout, 'what's that straight ahead?'—but he can't hear me over the sirens. We proceed to drive into the side of a supply truck. I'm thrown clear on impact and wind up in a brace for three months. Poor George, he loses his head, literally—severed at the neck. Guess I got the better bargain, eh?" He laughs his phlegmy laugh.

The sound relaxes your shoulders, makes you bolder. "If your nose was blown off," you say, pointing at the feature on his face, "what's that?"

Leaning forward with a grunt and a waft of cigarette, your grandfather hoists you into his lap. Up close, his eyes are marbles, shiny and wet, and his cheeks show pink veins under the skin. Hair sprouts between his eyes and out of his ears. His nose, you can see now, is a different hue, baloney left on the counter too long. He breathes through his mouth.

"Doctors rebuilt it using skin stripped from my backside," he says. "That's right, kiddo. Your old man's old man has an ass for a nose!"

His laugh now dissolves into a cough, and you feel him quake, lungs rattling like a blender filled with ice. He spits into a hankie with the letters CJF stitched in a corner.

"Dapper, eh?" he says, noticing your attention. "A man should always carry a pocket handkerchief. Or a gentleman should."

You nod.

"Touch it," he says, pointing at his own face. "Don't be afraid."

The nose is soft and wobbly, and the holes are slits, barely open.

"No cartilage up there. Sock me one, and I won't feel a thing. Never felt any pain, matter of fact—not even with a broken back."

"Were you a GI Joe in the war?" you ask.

"No GI Joes in the Canadian army. First-rate soldiers only. Finest combat troops in the world. Ask the Krauts if that's not the truth."

You say "Okay," but your shoulders tense up again.

"Your grandpa was an acting general by the end of '44. Retired a full colonel after two more years of bringing our troops home. Colonel Charlie Foran. That's me," he says, his gaze suddenly faraway. "And that's you, too."

You are pinching his nose and laughing so hard you are almost peeing when your father enters.

"How about this kid," your grandfather says. "A real asslicker. Will make a great officer someday, eh?"

But then, catching a look on his son's face, he drops you to the hardwood floor. You land on your knees—a sting, although you know better than to complain.

At lunch, your little brother Mike asks Shirley a dumb question. "Are you my grandma?" he says.

Shirley pauses for several seconds, and you take in her nice dress and earrings. She glances over at Grandpa Charlie, then down at her food. "If you want me to be, Mike," she finally says.

Your sister Debbie bangs her fork on her plate. "She is *not* our grandmother. She's just some nice lady."

"Now, now," your grandfather says.

In the car on the way home, your dad smokes cigarettes and steers with two fingers, which always makes Mom nervous. From the rear seat, you study the back of his head. The middle front seat, where you are often perched when the car is less full, is best for observing him. From there you can watch how he controls the wheel with his left hand and taps the dashboard with his right, a cigarette smoldering in the ashtray, Hank Williams or Glen Campbell on the radio. In the summer he wears short sleeves, his forearm muscles flexing to the music, the freckle archipelago rising and falling like a boat in heavy seas.

But today your father doesn't want to listen to the radio. He is quiet, maybe sad, though you can't figure out why. Hoping to cheer him up, you ask him to quiz his children on the ten provinces of Canada and fifty states of the USA, the fifteen prime ministers and thirty-seven presidents. He loves giving car quizzes.

"Not today, kiddo," he says.

After a moment, you ask your mom about handkerchiefs. "I want ones with my initials sewn on," you say.

"What's wrong with Kleenex?"

"Not dapper enough," you answer. "Especially for a gentleman."

"Hear that, Dave," your mom says. "Charlie thinks Kleenex aren't dapper enough for a gentleman."

Your father is silent, and no one says a word for the rest of the ride.

16

Until I wrote one for my father, I rarely read obituaries or "lives lived" columns. But in the aftermath of his passing, I found myself drawn to their headlines, and then to the key framing details—first and final days on earth, cause of death, testimonials of family and friends. The lives of men, especially, became of near-actuarial interest: heavyset men in their late fifties who'd held stressful jobs; heavyset men in their late fifties who looked, based on the photos, like passengers in their own bodies.

And yet, the newspaper obituary that affected me most was radically different from those accounts. MM had passed away after a two-year battle with an aggressive form of leukemia. She'd faced a "long and difficult road through her time with cancer," and was someone "beyond her years in love, determination and wisdom." Despite the illness, M was "rarely scared, rarely felt sorry for herself and always kept a playful sense of humor that brought joy and tears to many a moment." When out of hospital, she loved "the adventure of baking something new, tending her beautiful garden blossoms, and family boat rides to chase the sunset."

The notice included a photo: M sits on a couch, an arm draped over a pillow, her gaze far away. She is poised and thoughtful, as if preoccupied with a wise notion, her features accentuated by a shaved head. "We love you M," the notice ended, "baby unicorn, kitty, foal, baby elephant, baby tiger, and porcupine." MM died at age four.

Directly beneath MM in the newspaper that same day, separated by two solid lines of ink, was a shorter notice for JS, an economist with a distinguished career at the University of Toronto, where he taught for decades and published text-books on macroeconomic theory. He left behind three sons, among them a popular author. JS was ninety-six.

The illness that killed MM brought to mind my friend David Bierk, who fought leukemia for thirteen years. But MM's photo, and perhaps the music of her name, summoned a far older memory as well. I had a cousin named Murielle McCoy, who had died of cancer when I was a teenager. Though she lived most of her eighteen years in Blind River, the town in northern Ontario where my mother was born and raised, Murielle had spent several months in our home in suburban Toronto. More exactly, she'd stayed off and on in our base-ment, sleeping on the couch in the family room, while seeing doctors and receiving treatments. I also slept in the basement, a cramped bedroom with a window facing a neighbor's brick wall. My cousin and I had shared quarters for long periods during her time in our house; we couldn't avoid each other and exchanged a few words each day.

Then she died.

And I forgot about her.

Not only had I forgotten the details of my encounters with Murielle McCoy; her very existence, I now realized, had absented itself from my memory for at least two decades. Was this an example of how childhood trauma can vanish from adult recollection in order to protect a fragile self? Or, more likely, was it an instance of shame backpedaling from a room, closing the door softly behind itself and pretending it had never been there.

Murielle had been the second youngest of seven children born to Delisca and Tommy McCoy. Her name had confounded me as a child. Muriel was my mother's first name, and my cousin's mother, my Aunt Del, looked so much like her kid sister, Muriel Foran, that I sometimes mixed them up, especially from behind. More than once I hugged my aunt when I meant to hug my mother, inhaling the same scent; on several occasions I answered a phone call from "up north," only to wonder how my mother, watching TV downstairs, could also be on the far end of the line. It was confusing to my child mind: my aunt, whose voice and features and smell belonged to my mother, Muriel, had a daughter called Murielle, who looked a little like my own sister.

My cousin was never healthy. Her kidneys flowed in both directions, causing extreme weight gain and, it was believed, slowing her growth. The weight peeled off once surgeons repaired the kidneys, but she remained small for her age.

A couple of years later, when Murielle was fourteen and I was twelve, she was diagnosed with cancer of the pituitary, the probable cause of her stature. The diagnosis came late, and the cancer had already spread through her auditory and optic nerves. By age fifteen, Murielle was often in Toronto receiving treatments. When not in hospital, she was on our couch, in her pajamas, paging through copies of *National Geographic*. She was a tiny, raven-haired girl with a whispery voice, a hopeful smile and eyes the blue of a Rocky Mountain lake. She fixed her gaze on people for so long they had to look away. Or I had to, at least. I passed by my cousin to get to my bedroom. Also, to eat, walk to school, drive to hockey practice with my dad, ride my bike to the shopping mall where I cut grass and swept sidewalks. I passed by her to use the washroom at night, negotiating the dark and the creaky stairs. "Hi, Charlie," Murielle would say, her English faintly accented. Then she would giggle, and I would take two stairs per step, my gangly body—I grew six inches in as many months—barely managing not to stumble.

I couldn't talk to her. "Go talk to Murielle," my mother would say. "She's lonely." I did try telling her about school and hockey and working at a mall, and she was keen to listen, interrupting my monologues with "jeez" and "no kidding, eh"— words of encouragement in rural-Ontario speech. But it was all too strange: a teenager in pajamas in the family room; me in my underwear climbing the stairs to pee. Murielle did once confess her plans to marry Guy Lafleur, star of the Montreal

Canadiens. Hearing that, I invited her into my room, down a short corridor, and showed her the poster of my own hockey god, Jean Béliveau, taped to the back of the door. But another day she asked me to sit down and, folding her hands in her lap, like the nuns did at school, lowered her voice. She was worried. "About what?" I asked. Murielle blinked twice and bit her lip, her gaze boring a hole into my chest. "That I might not get better this time," she answered. I must have said something in return, but what I recall is looking away and, soon after, fleeing her presence.

A year later, she was back in the city for still further care, her hair gone and the bruises beneath her eyes livid, externalizing, I imagined, a fury she might not be aware of feeling. Fury at what? I dared not speculate. The eyes, too, had lost much of their calm, showing equal parts curiosity and hunger—a hunger, simply, to keep on living. Seeing this, I decided my cousin must be an actual nun. A penitent, the cloistered bride of Jesus, the pajamas her habit and bald head her veil, praying for both our venial and mortal sins, and her own eternal salvation, from the basement of a house in the suburbs. My elementary school, Blessed Trinity—BTS on our sweater crest—was run by a nun, Sister Anne-Marie. She wore a gold cross around her neck and carried a leather strap. Sometimes Sister Anne-Marie strapped the boys herself, but usually she made a teacher do it. I cried the first time I received five straps across each palm, turning them pink-purple, the same colour as the cheeks of my uncles when they were drinking beer.

There was a final desperate operation, then Murielle returned to Blind River. I can't recall if we said goodbye. My sister, Debbie, meanwhile, had been a generous and protective companion to our cousin. She mourned Murielle's death—of a heart attack, a tumor now in her brain—and held her memory dear.

I grew another three inches, reaching my adult height, and eventually met Jean Béliveau. As the decades passed, my aunts and uncles began to die, always the men first, including my Uncle Tommy. My Aunt Del followed, and one of their grandchildren battled childhood cancer. But the McCoy kids, now adults, and their families were doing fine, had always been doing fine.

Or so I blithely assumed until I read the death notice for MM, another child, and the name Murielle, along with my cousin's face—those blue eyes, the "jeezes" and "ehs," that long black hair and diminutive body, not quite a teenager's but no longer a child's—came flooding back. Eighteen years she lived. Eighteen years she experienced the beautiful earth. Sunrises and sunsets, snowfalls and lashing rains; cats on windowsills, tails curled, chattering with blue jays on nearby branches. Eighteen years she saw the unconditional love in her mother's gaze, until underlying worry formed clouds. Saw the vow to protect in her father's expression, until helplessness slumped his shoulders and bunched his hands into fists.

Eighteen years!

Isn't that an eternity? MM might have thought so. Likewise, the blue jay on the branch and cat on the windowsill. That I, fifty-seven when I read MM's obituary, felt sudden sadness for my lost cousin, and shame and dismay at forgetting about her, was . . . what? Pathetic. Shallow. A failure to see the B-I-G. Meriting five, no ten, straps per palm, the harder, the more painful—skin lacerated, flesh pink-purple—the better.

I asked my sister to help me reconstruct Murielle, and she did, in part by sharing a photograph she had safeguarded all that time. In the photo, our cousin leans against a kitchen counter. She wears a white dress with a blue-check pattern along the shoulders. A flower is pinned to her collar, suggesting a wedding to attend, or high-school dance. Around her neck is a pendant, around her wrist a chain. Murielle is smiling, excited and bashful, a happy teenager at the outset of an adventure, one she will long cherish. She is also *un petit lapin*, a baby raccoon and spindly-legged foal, gazing trustingly at the camera about to record, and then never forget, her urgent presence.

Looking at the newspaper column with MM's notice, I thought: So many lives lived. And so many lives—the overwhelming majority—undocumented and unrecorded. Before I had to write about my father, I had accepted this pitiless math. I might even have declared that *only* accounts of the most prominent people, lives of so-called distinction and import, merited the ink. For the rest of us, there was nothing compelling to share, at least with strangers. Certainly nothing that a novel, play or poem couldn't frame more elegantly and render more vividly. Individual lives, however crucial to those experiencing them, and to those in the immediate circle, come and go. Bodies too, never mind the warming smiles and hearty laughs, vigorous shapes and gaits. And things done are naturally undone. Names on graves cease being legible; headstones topple and crumble, become pure stone again. Birds find other spots to rest atop. Wind elides over cleared ground.

I'm Nobody, who are you?

Are you Nobody too?

I certainly thought so. And thought, too, of this poem by E.E. Cummings:

anyone lived in a pretty how town
(with up so floating many bells down)
summer winter autumn winter
he sang his didn't he danced his did.

Later, "anyone" falls in love with "noone" and lives happily for a while. But then the inevitable:

one day anyone died i guess
(and noone stooped to kiss his face)
busy folk buried them side by side
little by little and was by was

Then there was Samuel Beckett's *Waiting for Godot*, a play I took too much to heart too soon into adulthood, and which offered no consolation for being awake and self-aware on this "bitch of an earth," except black humor and strained companionship. Estragon, waiting for Godot to appear, obsesses over "all the dead voices" around him. His friend Vladimir admits he hears the voices in rustlings, and in the breeze.

VLADIMIR: What do they say?
ESTRAGON: They talk about their lives.
VLADIMIR: To have lived is not enough for them.
ESTRAGON: They have to talk about it.
VLADIMIR: To be dead is not enough for them.
ESTRAGON: It is not sufficient.

But then I changed my thinking. Shortly after I read about MM and resurfaced memories of Murielle McCoy, I began poring over accounts of Nobody, anyone and no one, all those dead voices still needing to talk. I sought out details about what these people had liked to eat and drink, do with their minds and bodies, what and whom they loved. And I found I had kind thoughts for every one of them. I was impressed, moved, humbled by what they/we abided and overcame, joys experienced and shared, sorrows endured without too much complaint or cruelty; and, foremost, by the love they/we managed to give and receive, each gesture, large or small, hopeful and defiant—in mute protest, perhaps, against the aloneness

wired into our natures and the obscurity, nullity even, awaiting our ends.

Now I read obituaries and "lives lived" columns every day,
and I can't stop.

17

In June 2018, six months after my father passed away, I gave a commencement address to university students. This is part of what I said:

"Here is how it sometimes feels being an adult.

You are driving down a fast highway in a fast car. Like everyone else on the road, you're traveling alone. The day is clear, no snow or sleet, fog or rain, and spacing between vehicles is decent, allowing you to safely look left, look right, for a full second at a time.

In the vehicle beside you is a middle-aged man belting out 'Single Ladies.' Though you can't hear him sing, he is making gestures that you recognize as a truncated version of the dance moves—head dip, walk like an Egyptian, point to ring finger—from the Beyoncé video. In the next car, a woman is gesticulating to someone—either a person on her Bluetooth, or the Irish setter in the passenger seat. Still another driver in an SUV is eating noodles with chopsticks, spilling them over the steering wheel, and a guy in a pickup truck is pretending not to be texting. He drifts across the line, overcorrects back across the other line, still glancing down at his lap.

Erratic behavior abounds. Cars roar past you at well over the speed limit, mostly young men grim with unconscious death wishes. One driver sobs and wipes her nose on her sleeve while managing to keep both hands firmly on the wheel. She drives too slowly. There are many forlorn people out today, and you worry one of them will do something rash. Helpless to help them, you can only hope they take the next exit ramp, saving you from witnessing a solo crash or getting tangled up in their multi-vehicle despair.

But on the fast highway in your fast car, you also begin to notice faces, and to recognize them. There is the woman who resembles your sister-in-law from your first marriage, the one you watched reality TV with, both of you howling at the silly things humans said and did. You miss her more than you miss your own ex-spouse—a lot more, in fact. Or there's the face of the employee you had to let go, although he was a good guy and had two kids and a mortgage. Losing a job after forty can be a blow, and the suicide rates for men of a certain age . . . What became of him, you wonder, and you suddenly hope he is okay, wherever he landed.

Or, speaking of loss, how about the driver in the red car who could be your sister's best friend, the one you had a crush on at university. Your sister lost track of the friend over the decades, but you haven't stopped thinking about her, not exactly. Deny it up and down—and you would, if pressed, and not just with your wife—but you would have been good together. There was real chemistry there. A natural fit. Say it, why not: the woman whose face is like the woman in the red car was 'The One.' What an idiot you were back then, blowing your best chance at deeper happiness. And, worse, you are still an idiot today.

Or, speaking of regrets, how about the guy in the roofing-company van, a vehicle that doesn't seem highway safe, with a fender or even a wheel likely to come off. He could be—no, wait, he *is*—your good buddy from high school, thirty years ago. That guy was funny and smart, reckless and messed up. Had divorced parents. An abusive stepdad. Trouble with grades, teachers, authority, police. Smoked a lot of weed and hash and, twice in your presence, snorted cocaine. Wore too much real rage on his face and body, forever needing, seeking, walls to punch or just slam into. By Grade Eleven you were distancing yourself from him, sensing he was going to pop, and you didn't want to be around when it happened. You had an argument over something and fled the friendship like a building up in flames. Not long after, he quit school. You heard he drifted north to plant trees and then out west to work in the oil fields. You heard he did a stretch in prison and was spotted by another high-school buddy living rough in the east end.

Is that really your friend in the van? It sure looks like him. Truth be told, you didn't think he'd make it to forty, with the wounds he carried.

Then there is the octogenarian in a car they stopped manu-facturing in the last century, a car that should be banned from major highways. Take a closer look: it's your own dad, whom you never forgave for leaving your mom when you were a child, and who is now a sickly old man, lonely and bitter. There's been zero contact between you in ages. Meaning you've no idea really if he even *is* lonely and bitter, which he ought to be. And to hell with him still, the prick! But then you see the prick's son edging closer in the rearview mirror. Yes, there *you* are, a quarter-century younger, riding the back bumper and flashing your high beams. Get a load of that guy: thin and coiled, features lit by callow dreams, ambition and sex keeping his foot on the pedal, sights set on what is directly in front and most easily conquered.

One thing you know for sure. Among all the drivers on the highway today, he is the one you do *not* wish to meet.

You see these people in their cars, and they see you in your car, and maybe you ask: Okay, what happened to us? But you are all headed for different exit ramps, and in your moving vehicles there is no safe means of communicating any desire, however vague and fleeting, to connect. And here's another hard truth: you don't know these other drivers. They only remind you of people you do know, or did once, including your own regrettable younger self. So you drive on solo, another day done.

That is how it sometimes feels being an adult."

In my speech, I continued: "The stories I've told are not mine. They're a composite of stories I've seen or heard or imagined.

But the failures in my own life that haunt me are nearly all related to my deciding to opt out of contact with people I could have, should have, stayed connected with. At the very least, people whom I should have made greater effort to acknowledge as being around me, part of me, their struggles and sorrows identical to my own." Then: "You should know that everyone has trouble with the business of being in close, constant proximity with everyone else, and not being sure how to behave." It is our shared condition, I concluded, and our shared predicament.

My talk did not go over well. Fixating on vehicular alienation and failed relationships was probably a mistake for a commencement address. Likewise, portraying adulthood as a grind, stepping on the same life-lesson rake over and over, resulting, apparently, in permanent brain injury. Several students, passing by me to collect their degree from the university chancellor, offered kind words. One even put her hand on my arm and said, "It's going to be okay." I suspect I reminded her of her father, or any bewildered adult in her sphere. I suspect I reminded many graduates of their parents. Intending to tell a cautionary tale, I had served as one instead. Maybe, I consoled myself, that was of some help?

I had drafted, but then put aside, an alternative address. In part it read:

Adulthood can sometimes feel like a string of one-night affairs. But instead of a single evening of friction, each experience lasts about six months. Each, in the moment, is full of satisfaction

*and meaning. Each also portends happy change and—at last—
confident direction.*

*For instance: For six months you are in love—love of the
consuming, never-felt-anything-like-this variety. The person has
lifted your heart up, drawn you out of shadow, shown you the
path. Or you make a baby. A baby! For six months your eyes are
opened to the universe, the flood of light across the field. No more
midnight sob-fests. No more anxious waits for dawn. Or you get
the new job. Not a job—the job, the one you dreamed of and
fought for. It is the career cap, the life changer, the face in the
mirror that is, finally, the face you will proudly own. At least, it
feels this way for half a year. Almost, although not quite, as full
of meaning as making that baby or falling in crazy love.*

*And those are the big-ticket items, the illusions worth delud-
ing yourself over. How about the new condo or house? Four
months of friction, tops. Or the flash car that has you feeling
sleek and sexy? Ninety days, at the outside. The bespoke suit and
Prada bag, business-class ticket and five-star hotel? A month, if
lucky. After that, it is the organic wild cod flown in from the west
coast, the 1957 Bowmore single malt from Islay, the dark choco-
late by Amedei. Give those a week, if your nature is sunny, or
twenty-four hours, if you're like most of us. Then the satisfaction, the satiation, drains away, sure as water down a drain, and
hunger and thirst creep back in. Along with disappointment. The
nag of desire.*

*Until, that is, the next drink or meal, holiday or car, house or
job, come along. Happy days, or maybe weeks, of friction. Better*

still, the babies, so adorable and fresh, and the sweeter, more
agreeable lover. Six months of bliss, here we all come.

I had planned to end this version with the famous Albert
Einstein quote: "A human being is a part of the whole, called by
us 'Universe,' a part limited in time and space. He experiences
himself, his thoughts and feelings, as something separated
from the rest—a kind of optical delusion of his consciousness.
This illusion is a prison for us, restricting us to our personal
desires and to affection for a few people nearest to us. Our task
must be to free ourselves from this prison by widening our
circles of compassion to embrace all living beings and the
whole of nature."

For decades those words were pinned to a bulletin board
beside my writing desk. As explained by a great mind, a meaningful existence seemed so clear: the challenge of a lifetime,
simply framed. To escape the shabby prison of the self, and our
disastrous relations with the rest of the planet, we need only
"widen our circles of compassion." How to go about this? By
getting out of our miserable heads. Getting out and staying out.

But even with the Einstein quote, would the graduating
class of 2018 have liked my alternative speech any better? I was
in a mood, heavy of heart, head and spirit; and heavy, for all to
see, of jowl and gut. "You're looking more and more like your
dad," people had been saying to me, thinking, I am sure, of that
jowl, that gut. "Not for trying," I usually replied, thinking of
head, heart, spirit. Such a comment earned puzzled expressions, which I ignored—just as I was ignoring concerned looks

from my wife about my appearance and manner, the fatigue that kept my feet in cement.

This conversation was private. I thought of two generations of men in a fast car racing down a fast highway, no exits in sight, brakes failing or already failed. That sounded about right.

18

You have no one to ask for permission. Your father is in Europe, fighting the Nazis. Your older sister, Barb, is at summer camp. Your mom lives in your family's apartment, where you lived until recently, but you haven't talked to her in ages and aren't allowed to tell the operator to please connect you to Queen1407. Aunt Jean told you and Barb: "Leave your mother be for now. She has to get better." So now you are both staying with Aunt Jean and Uncle Harry, in a house that is miles away from Sandy Hill, until your mom gets better—which, you already know, means not sneaking her first drink before lunch. "She'll never stop," you heard your aunt tell your uncle. "Poor her. Poor them, especially."

But you are no poor boy, and you don't think your sister is a poor girl. You need to speak with your dad. Several times you've tried, secretly picking up the phone and requesting that the operator put you through to Colonel Charlie Foran, stationed in England, or maybe Belgium. Though most of those women tell you to get off the line, an older-sounding operator asks you when you last saw your father or talked to him. "I was seven," you answer. When you reply to her next question—you say you are ten now, almost a man—the woman's voice softens. "Honey," she says, "everything's going to be okay."

Your dad says that too—or used to. He would stand behind your chair at the kitchen table and squeeze your shoulders too hard. "You okay, kiddo?" he would ask. Your mother never touches you or Barb; she pulls back from people as if they are on fire. Now, every day, you stare at the photo of the colonel in full regalia that you brought from the apartment, although you weren't permitted to bring the lamp in your bedroom, the one that casts animal silhouettes onto the wall. But you still see those images in your dreams—rabbit, deer, moose, bear— along with officers in trench coats and leather boots, pistol sashes and hats with insignia. Sometimes you dream of both animals and men. The streets of Ottawa are sure full of soldiers, and while it is foolish—Colonel Foran is in Europe fighting the Nazis—your mouth goes dry whenever you pass by one displaying a crown and two stars.

Asking permission from your Aunt Jean and Uncle Harry to walk from their house in Alta Vista to another uncle's home in Rockcliffe Park isn't something you will do—ever. You're still mad at them for complaining in front of you about the "arrangement," and how they weren't meant to be doing the "heavy lifting." It is true that John Foran, the other uncle, promised his youngest brother Charlie—that's your dad—to look after Barb and Dave while he sorted out the Krauts. "Hell," Uncle John said, right in front of you and your sister, "the kids can come live with us, if it proves too much for Ruthie. Anything for the family." "Anything," it seems, except even one single thing, such as inviting the "kids" to their house for Christmas or Thanksgiving, or calling to see how you and Barb, or your sick mom Ruthie, are doing all these months—no, all these *years*—later. You've rehearsed that call a hundred times. "She's not doing too well, Uncle John," you will say to him. "And can I please play with my cousin Dick, like you said I could?"

You set off mid-morning, a map of the route, copied from a city guide, in your pocket. You are a soldier parachuted behind enemy lines, the map—guiding the soldier to the bridge he must blow up—hidden in your sock. It is August, and the sky is high and cloudless, hazy from the heat. You are red-haired and freckled and wearing no cap. Following Bank Street to the river is straightforward. Same for crossing the gleaming white bridge, the Rideau green and sluggish between the arches. Though you could save a mile by staying on the east side of the river, you head for downtown. Sandy Hill sits between the bridge and Lower Town, and you wouldn't mind walking by the apartment where you usually live. Not stopping in; just walking by. Your mother is probably home, keeping out of the sun that so disagrees with her complexion, and flipping through magazines. Sipping a cool drink. Humming to the radio. You know her favorite song as well as she does. *Do you think I'll remember/How you looked when you smile?/Only forever/That's puttin' it mild.*

You hum the tune now, hearing her voice wobble, trying to hold the melody, which is easy.

Riverdale Avenue takes you to Main Street. A streetcar rumbles past and the Peace Tower peals twelve bells. Thanks to gas rationing, you can walk down the center of most streets without being honked at. You like doing that. You admire St. Pat's high school, where you will probably end up in two years, and then skirt along the eastern flank of Sandy Hill. No one spots you. No one sees the soldier executing his secret mission. Thirsty—it is boiling out now—you stop at Sandelman's for a Coke.

"Long time, no see," Mr. Sandelman says.

"I'm on a mission," you reply.

"Groceries for your mother?"

"I can't say."

Three soldiers enter the shop. Your heart pounds, despite that they are noncommissioned men, two of them with no stripes at all. They ask for Woodbines and Cokes, and wipe their brows, khaki shirts soaked through.

"My dad smokes Woodbines," you say, straightening your posture. "He's a full colonel."

The soldier with the stripe looks at you. "What division?" he asks.

"First infantry. But he's at HQ."

"An Alder-big-shot, eh?"

"He's in England, I think," you answer, confused.

"Leave the kid alone," Mr. Sandelman says.

"My mom likes Chesterfields," you tell them. "I have to go see my father's brother. We talk war stuff."

"You go," one of the soldiers says.

You don't think of walking by the apartment now. Strathcona Park offers some shade, the trees' dark canopies and spruce needles releasing a ripe scent, like your dad's cologne. You remember the cologne, or imagine you do. You must remember! Colonel Foran would approve of your mission so far. Okay, maybe not the stop for a Coke, but everything else. "Textbook soldiering," the Colonel would say. "Top drawer." Your sister does a funnier imitation of him. Puffs her chest and drops her voice, drags on a phantom cigarette. "Jesus-h-Christ, Ruthie. Not in front of the kids!" She was older when your father went away; she has clearer memories of him, and of you as a family. You miss Barb too. Why so long at summer camp?

On St. Patrick Bridge, which you could blow up if you had the dynamite, you decide that you should have stuffed your Royals baseball cap into your pocket. Steam rises from the river. Sweat stings your eyes. You study the soggy map, confirming the name of the long street—Springfield—that will take you up into Rockcliffe Park, where John and Winifred Foran live. Once you have memorized it, you tear the map up and release the bits into the Rideau—more top-drawer soldiering.

The final half hour is pure grit. You really should have worn your cap. You really should have used your other nickel to buy a Hershey bar. You feel light, a helium balloon ready to climb the sky. You also feel heavy, like you did that time you caught fever and lay in bed for days, a compress to your forehead and your mother rubbing Vicks VapoRub onto your chest. The burn. The smell. And wait a second: she touched you! She had to, of course. You feel close to crying now, although you can't think why, and pinch a prickly bush to stanch the emotion. Raising your arm, you watch the blood ride down the inside of your finger and spread across your palm, not feeling a thing.

As you turn at last onto Maple Lane, a block of brick homes with garages and lawns, you remember Uncle John. Once he ruffled your hair and called you "Red." You try remembering Aunt Winifred. She, as best you can recall, never spoke to you or Barb, nor pretended to be friends with your mom or "big-shot" dad. But you remember your cousin Dick. You remember how you used to play together. Dick likes—liked—you. He'll be happy to see your face.

You stand before the front door. It is brown, made of wood, with both a knocker and a bell.

Did you break a vase in their house when you were five or six? Tip it off a coffee table, no rug to absorb the fall? The incident comes back to you, a rush of blood to the head. But so what? Kids break vases. Adults, you are beginning to sus-pect, break everything else.

A voice keeps you from retreating to the street. It is your father, sweeping into your room and pulling back the curtains. "Wake up!" Colonel Foran says. "Don't sleep so much!"

You tell yourself you're not scared, and don't need to pee—or not too badly. You even hum, following your mother's shaky melody line. *How long would it take me/To be near if you beckon?/ Off hand I could figure/Less than a second.*

You ring the doorbell.

19

For as long as I can remember, I've been fascinated by ruins. Temples, churches, burial mounds and cemeteries, amphitheaters, stadiums, city walls and aqueducts, even just ordinary buildings, houses, barns and sheds: my eye is drawn to their beauty and humility, the evidence of lives lived and lives forgotten nestled within their rubble. During the period when I was mourning the death of my father—and my own younger, more purposeful self—I doubled down on this fascination, largely via the Internet. At the same time, my appetite for learning almost anything, in the hope of better understanding a few things, as though for future career advancement and personal growth, also expanded. If these impulses seemed contradictory, even in conflict, one raising a gaze to the sky and the other lowering a foot into the grave, I didn't care. Or I didn't notice, being myself in conflict, contradictory.

For instance, I realized one day that I didn't know whether Carthage existed outside of history books. I associated the fabled city with Saint Augustine, the fourth-century theologian so foundational to Christianity and Western philosophy. His works, especially *Confessions* and *City of God*, had been essential reading at my Catholic college. I googled his name. Augustine of Hippo was a Numidian, born in present-day northern Algeria, and served as a priest in the town of Hippo, now called Annaba. Carthage lay a hundred miles further east along the Mediterranean coast of Africa, in the modern-day nation of Tunisia. The original Phoenician city, a rival to Rome, was sacked and burned by the Romans at the close of the Third Punic War in 160 BCE. The Carthage where Augustine had misspent his early adulthood five centuries later—"give me chastity and continence," he wrote, "but not yet"—was rebuilt by the same conquerors who had destroyed it earlier.

That Carthage eventually fell to invaders as well, and the city went to ground for a millennium. Archeologists began excavating temples, baths, roads and aqueducts in the 1870s. Today the lost metropolis of Queen Dido and, later, Augustine of Hippo was a tourist spot in a suburb of Tunis. The artificially protected harbor had vanished long ago, but the distinctive circular basin was still visible two thousand years later.

Called a "Cothon," the harbor is typical of the genius of the Roman war machine. There were many re-creations available online, and I studied them, comparing models and settings. I also read more about the excavations, the Punic Wars, Saint Augustine, and Queen Dido, who may not have existed. Two pleasurable hours passed by—click, click, click of the mouse.

My immersion wasn't only digital. How come, I suddenly wondered, I hadn't known about the ruins of Carthage, and had never been to Tunisia or Algeria? This appeared another lapse in my education, like my failure to read *Confessions* or *City of God* as an undergrad, rather than simply keeping the books on my bedroom shelf, in case a Catholic girl visited. Could I read them now? Get to those countries? I investigated flights and visas and scanned the accounts of travelers. A listing for a public lecture on Augustine called "The Search for Wisdom" turned up in my inbox, and I reserved a spot. I also ordered *Confessions* from a bookseller—my college copy went missing in the 1990s—and daydreamed about how I could alternate reading Augustine with the *Aeneid*, which features Dido in the early chapters, while touring Carthage and Hippo, perhaps in the company of my wife and our adult daughters.

Would there be elephants? I didn't see any photos of elephants on these websites. But I did recall the story of the Carthaginian general, Hannibal, who had used the animals to sneak over the Alps in winter and attack Rome. I had faint memories of starting the *Aeneid* a couple of times, of finding it a struggle. A little research assuaged my guilt: Virgil spent half his poetic lines telling a rambling tale lifted, for the most part, from Homer's *Iliad,* and the rest propagandizing for empire.

But then everyone, I acknowledged, must serve somebody. That random thought compelled me to dig up a CD of *Slow Train Coming*, the passionate, raggedy Bob Dylan album from 1979, and listen to "Gotta Serve Somebody."

Later that same day, having listened to covers of "Gotta Serve Somebody" online, most delivered with greater conviction and musicality than Dylan brought to his own composition, I started on a larger project of comparing versions of iconic songs. Bruce Springsteen's "Atlantic City" was an interesting example. None of the half dozen covers I could find on YouTube captured the grit and midnight weariness of the original, despite the musicians likely being closer to the source material, via their own experiences and identities, than he had been. "Atlantic City" came out of Springsteen fully realized, every note and lyric inevitable, if not traceable. As such, no one could understand better than he the emotional space the song must inhabit, the tone it needed to strike and hold—regardless of whether he had "lived" the story.

From Bruce Springsteen, I drifted to Indonesian gamelan music. How did those currents intersect? I had suddenly remembered listening to *Darkness on the Edge of Town* in my bedroom the second summer after its release. The year was 1979; I was eighteen. Each night I put the record on, inviting Springsteen's sad, often desperate story songs to wind down my waking thoughts. I would slip Side A or B onto the stereo beside my bed, cut the lights and float. The receiver panel glowed blue, and I lay on my side facing it, buoyed by musical phosphorescence. Usually, I drifted into a happy sleep before the needle returned to the arm. That was for the best. If I was still awake when the stereo went dark, the room, previously a vessel of words and music and caressing light, would splinter and plunge into an oceanic darkness, the depths uncharted.

Decades later, traveling with my family in Bali, I bought a CD of gamelan. The music was spare and haunting, syncopated melodies in a pentatonic loop, like rain on a tin roof during monsoon. When we returned home, our youngest daughter, then five years old, found her first months in a new bedroom to be fraught, monsters in the closet and intruders at the window. Her mother and I suggested she fall asleep to music, and after auditioning more predictable selections, she gave the gamelan a try. The melodies dissolved her anxieties; perhaps they washed away her thoughts the way rain on a roof can. As a teenager, Claire would shake her head in disbelief that she had ever taken solace in such music. But she had. Even better, she might take such solace again, I told her, life being all about changes, often surprising and nearly always positive, whether sought out or, as is most often the case, visited upon you.

Remembering this story, I scoured my music collection, and then the Internet, for the CD from Bali, without success. But the search did lead to further reading about the tradition of gamelan, most notably its centrality to Wayang, the Indonesian puppet theater that retells tales from Hindu mythology. Checking out clips of Wayang performances online—we had taken our girls to a performance for children on that same Bali trip—got me thinking about a novel I once read called *The Year of Living Dangerously*. A film was made of the book, starring Mel Gibson and Sigourney Weaver as lovers in Jakarta during a coup. The Indonesian who brought them together, played by the American actress Linda Hunt, recast their romance as Wayang, using those shadow puppets to convey the mythic underlays. A conventional trope, nicely done, or so I recalled. But I hadn't seen the movie in twenty-five years and doubted I could abide its synthesizer-heavy soundtrack now. I also worried the story might be more colonial in its gaze than I remembered, the developing world an "exotic"—indeed, "dangerous"—setting for white people to enact their dramas.

And so on. Literally: on and on. Until I slept. Increasingly, my appetite wasn't confined to art and artists. One afternoon, for instance, I went for a drive in the countryside. Plaques noting incidents from local history dotted the roads, and I stopped to read them, using Google searches to learn more on the spot. On that ride I also listened to a radio documentary about the Large Hadron Collider, the particle accelerator buried underground along the border between Switzerland and France. The Hadron "smashes" atoms to replicate the energies of the universe moments after the Big Bang. This, in turn, helps us understand dark matter. Though I understood neither dark matter nor smashing atoms and doubted pulling off the road again to google these concepts would make much difference, I found the documentary so compelling that I could not help myself. As compelling as, another night, I found a TV show about comfort animals, among them miniature ponies in Australia that are permitted onto commercial flights. Likewise, a two-part radio series about the sewers of Paris and—a

different night again—podcasts about the surveillance state
in China, digital disruptions to economies, concussions in
professional sports.

And on and on and on. Until I slept.

After he retired, my father had become obsessed with
hardware stores. He went missing in them for hours, wandering the aisles and chatting with employees, comparing types
and grains of woods, styles of windows and doors, brands of
band saws and lathes. He would step out to buy nails to craft
his bird houses and reappear hours later, dazed and happy,
unable to explain how he had spent the time. "Puttering," he
called it, his smile abashed. His family were amused and
ascribed the quirk to age and excess leisure. We only wished
he carried a cell phone and didn't already have an abundance
of tools on his workbench.

But then the same thing happened to me with super-
markets. It began around the time my father took permanently
ill. I would step out with a short list of ingredients for dinner,
ten minutes of targeted shopping, and find myself pondering the whiskered fish from Sri Lanka, the tubs of feta from
Greece and Parmesan wheels that could have fallen off Roman
chariots, the rows of lethal chili sauces with similar tastes—
or better, stings—but different countries of origin: Thailand,
Malaysia, Taiwan, China. Also, the shelves of olive oils, their
brine the gold of mustard fields in late summer. And the
Asian vegetables, once a culinary report from trans-Pacific

travels, now grown north of the city. Never mind the jars of curries and chutneys from the Indian subcontinent, or the cans of Lebanese stuffed grape leaves. I started getting calls in the store on my cell phone. I had been gone ninety minutes? Impossible. Loved ones were concerned for my safety. They were also hungry and—frankly—annoyed.

Saint Augustine, whom I could not have appreciated in my twenties, wrote in the *Confessions* of the "various forces at play in one soul," and of how much easier it is to count the hairs on a man's head than "his feeling, the movements of his heart." Yet here I was, tracking a spike in curiosity and openness within myself, a keenness for any insight into the workings of things. It was a late-midlife arousal, erotic if not sexual, a desire to be more and more of the world, in the world, however passingly and amateurishly, and so perhaps see the connections, the connectedness, that must be the quiet counter to the industrial noise of everyday time.

Augustine also observed that humans will "wonder at the heights of mountains, at the huge waves of the sea ... at the vast compass of the ocean, at the circular motions of the stars, and then pass by themselves without wondering." But I did not believe I was avoiding mirrors. Instead, I was more and more in love, and it was the Big Love, as my friend David Bierk might have phrased it. In Big Love with this place and space; in Big Love with my tiny spot within it, my silly, imperfect attempts at comprehending. Big Love wasn't about finding out how a fish from Sri Lanka wound up in a supermarket in Toronto, let alone the purpose of the Hadron Collider. It was about curiosity and astonishment; it was even about supplication. Maybe it was about—what would my father have thought of this notion?—starting to let go.

20

In early autumn I took a road trip with my mother and eldest daughter. The trip followed my first annual checkup with the cardiologist I had been assigned fourteen months before, after a battery of inconclusive tests. Additional tests had been done in preparation for the appointment, but they too were inconclusive, and when the cardiologist asked about my health, I admitted to feeling neither better nor worse than a year ago. "Just older," I said. "And my father died," I added, hardly medical news. The doctor, a busy, no-nonsense person who saw many patients every day, most of whom I probably resembled— i.e., men over a certain age, in a certain shape, with certain proclivities—quit staring at his screen. He swiveled his stool to gaze at me instead, a look that traveled head to foot, dispassionate as a hangman sizing up the condemned. Although I secretly wondered if the cardiologist remembered who I was, he knew his business. Or better, he knew *what* I was and my *kind* of body only too well.

"You don't look right," he finally said.

"Tell me about it," I said.

"I can't just yet," he answered. "But I have a hunch." He ordered yet more tests.

In the car, tracking the eastern shoreline of a great lake and advancing deeper into the bush, the trees still in color but their hues now muted, I asked my mother about my father's history with heart disease. Despite a laundry list of risky personal habits—an allergy to exercise, a passion for fatty foods, heavy smoking into his forties—he hadn't experienced any real problems until the age of seventy-five. Then he had a triple bypass and carried on for another decade.

We were headed north on a six-hour drive to Blind River, the town where Muriel Fallu was from, and where Murielle McCoy had died. I hadn't been there in decades, and neither of our daughters had visited their grandmother's birthplace. But I remembered childhood summers in Blind River among my *tantes et oncles, cousins et cousines*, long sunny days of swimming and fishing and short muggy nights sleeping atop sheets in cramped houses stuffed with relations, many of them around my age. As with my father's family, the grandparents were absent—in this instance, both were already deceased, their lives shortened by illness. The ten other Fallu sisters, however, now reconfigured as Lemieuxs and Brunos, McCoys, Dions and Proulxs, knew and cared about their city relations, even though we lived far away most of the year and, with the exception of my mother, did not speak French very well.

One boyhood memory of Blind River I held especially close. Near the cluster of houses owned by those uncles and aunts was a hill dubbed "the mountain" by locals. I passed July and August days wandering it alone or with cousins. For a boy from the suburbs, the mountain was an adventure park, full of things amazing, mysterious and scary. Beside the river was an abandoned building, firepits still smoldering from nocturnal parties and hobos sleeping rough. I came upon lovers seeking privacy and men drinking out of paper bags, along with shell-casings and bottles, usually smashed. Ant colonies fanned across the limestone covering the hilltop, and snakes slithered in the cracks. The snakes were garter, harmless and shy, but I was told to be alert for massasauga rattlers, their heads triangular. Most summers I stayed with my Aunt Marie and Uncle René in a house that backed onto the southern slope of the mountain. Wolves howled at night and there were reports of bears. I wouldn't have minded meeting a bear, just like my father had, and carried a stick in case.

Only one warning was issued about the mountain: "Stay away from the mineshafts." Companies had dug shafts up there earlier in the century, hoping to find mineral seams. They didn't; or, if they did, the seams were not rich enough, and instead the companies left behind detritus, holes sealed with timber planks that had since rotted. A couple of the holes were deep, and a cousin told me how a boy, jumping on a wooden cover, had crashed through. They fished his corpse out the next day.

That same cousin, called Aurel, ten years old to my eight, dared me to attempt what had killed that boy. About the size of the tabernacle in our church, the mineshaft cover was partially collapsed, likely from other kids testing it as well. Aurel went first, stepping onto the planks and bouncing up and down, both his feet lifting off. I could scarcely watch, especially his face, which wore the defiant grin of a son being beaten by his father. My turn came. Not wanting to show fear either, I committed one leg to the cover, and then the other. I wobbled, nearly tipping into the open part, but slowly righted myself. Soon I was also jumping, a feeble piston compared to Aurel, only my heels lifting, never my toes.

Even so, I had my first experience of terror and exhilaration in tandem that day, along with a disruption of my field of vision—objects turned jittery and blurred. That, as much as the squeaking of the planks, made me nauseous, a metal taste flooding my mouth. Next, we dropped onto our stomachs, calling down into the blackness. "Hello!" we called. Heart pummeling, I waited for a reply from below.

Back then, I thought these holes were called "mind" shafts. It made sense, and when I learned the truth, I never told anyone my mistake. After all, in our church in Toronto there was that hole above the tabernacle, dug into the sky to allow God to descend to earth for mass and then ascend back up afterward. The ceiling around the shaft was painted white and light poured down from it without fail, dust motes swirling within the beam. Besides being God's elevator for visits, the shaft was also, I decided, his mind—warm and radiant, a perpetual energy. Thinking about God as pure light made me happy. Thinking about the "mind" shafts in Blind River, even with the dead boy at the bottom, made me happy too.

Happiness for a child, I once read, is existential, not psychological. A child is happy not because of any one thing she or he does. A child is happy because she lives in the universe of talking animals and doorways into Narnia. A child is happy because he is attuned to sensation and wonderment, and innately receptive to change. A child, as a kept creature, is safe to jump atop mine shafts, and never fall in. A child does not understand loss, or perhaps mortality. A child is not yet us.

Childhood, Annie Dillard wrote, is something we wake up from, "piecemeal over the years." We notice the process, and soon realize that one day we will be "awake continuously," and never free again. Free from what? Our adult selves, Dillard explains, in so many words. We will never again be free from the "I" that keeps us good or fair or dreary or awful company to the grave. All that time together! All that time beyond our time as well, time that we will never experience— a sadness we can't quite measure or account for.

For much of my adult life I had been thinking about childhood and this process of waking up for good, contrasting existential and psychological happiness. Until recently, I had accepted as fact the dichotomy between who—and how—we were in the world as children, and how—and who—we were in the world as adults. But now I was wondering if I'd got it wrong, at least about how fixed anyone is, in any particular time. These past few years, for instance, I had experienced moments and lingered in spaces that felt neither childhood-existential nor adult-psychological. Possibly I had been having those moments, being in those spaces, all along, and not noticing; more likely, they were new to who I was now—in my mid- and then my late fifties, not looking or feeling quite right, with my father dying, then deceased. These were apprehensions, in effect, triggered neither by almost stepping off cliffs as a young adult nor falling into mind shafts as a boy. Rather, they happened through lifting. Releasing. Seeing, in the scrubbed clarity, what was right there, and saying *aahh*.

Some examples.

I am lying on my back in a bamboo grove, the stalks towering and clustered so that sunlight only penetrates in flickers. The earth pillow-like. The scent of jasmine. Gazing up at the sway, the flickering light, the murmur of bamboo on bamboo, I am off the ground, almost no weight to my body, the sun waiting to embrace me.

I am watching paper lanterns climb a night sky. The lanterns are conical, a candle lit within each, the flames illuminating cream-colored shells and providing thrust. Upward they soar, through a lower tier of gray-black into a clearer tier of blue-black. Above that is a dome of stars, where the lanterns are bound, to co-join with other pinpoints of light—or light from a million years ago. I track their ascent, head crooked and neck strained, until I too drift up, no ceiling or frame to hold me down.

I am wandering a Japanese temple dedicated to Jizo, guardian of children, passing row upon row of babies, some wearing bibs, others wearing bonnets. Their faces serene and heads shaven, hands cupping bowls for alms or folded in prayer. These are the "water children," effigies to infants who died, or else were stillborn, miscarried, aborted. Being made of stone, the creatures are as rooted to the earth as death is to life. But I am less attached. The longer I walk the temple grounds, battling a desire to touch a cheek or take a hand, the less sure I am of my own rootedness. When their downcast eyes find mine, shy smiles in response to my attention, I feel it again: the soaring, the release.

Was *aahh* the correct sound to describe these sensations? A spontaneous exhalation, drawn straight from the chest and lungs—it felt right. Yet I, a writer, surely should have had words for this sound, these sensations. I told myself these "apprehensions"—an inadequate term—should not have been so difficult to describe.

And, I told myself, they shouldn't have been so difficult to sustain.

The trip to Blind River with my mother and daughter proved a test of exactly how difficult it was to sustain a state of transcendent apprehension. There was a family gathering. We sat among a dozen relations, eating and drinking and fielding comparisons of Muriel to her late sister Del, of Anna

to two cousins of mine she had never met, and of me, invari-
ably, to my father—and also to my brother, a resemblance
I saw more clearly. Eventually my daughter and I slipped out
to walk the mountain. The day was fine; my heart and head
were good. I was keen to rediscover the mine/mind shafts
after so long and feel the thrum of the universe rumbling
beneath a northern town. Doing so in the company of one of
my children would make the experience all the sweeter.

As expected, the mountain of my boyhood was a hill,
small and scruffy. Less expected was how quickly I turned to
brooding about my mother's family, a rare shift away from the
paternal. But the story of my late cousin Reina, daughter of
my godmother, Marie, gripped my thoughts and would not
relinquish them. Teenage Reina had doted over her city
nephew those summers a half century ago, treating me like
a small prince, loving me as her own. She'd had a troubled
life, including an abusive marriage to a police officer later
convicted of two murders, and believed responsible for other
terrible crimes. Earlier in my career, I had decided I was interested in the pathologies of violent men and wrote a magazine
piece about the cop and my cousin, then a recluse in an
apartment on the west side of the hill. The piece was a mistake. I learned nothing writing it and doubted readers learned
anything reading one more account of male sociopathy. The
hours spent interviewing my gentle, damaged cousin had
made me feel voyeuristic. Worse, I saw too late that I'd had no
right to interrogate her and then use the material in ways she

probably wouldn't have understood or appreciated. Only a heartless mercenary would have done that to a supposedly beloved relation.

On the hilltop now with my daughter, I fumed about the cop, this man who had harmed so many people, and how dismal it was that the Wikipedia entry for Blind River—drawing, perhaps, from that magazine article published a while back—mentioned him by name, as though he were a distinguished citizen. My daughter and I found no covered mineshafts, but I still fell into one, the "mind" kind. Soon I was brooding too about my cousin Aurel, who had first tested the wooden cover. I had worshipped Aurel and followed him around, doing whatever he did. He grew up to be a heavy smoker with an alcohol problem and died in his early fifties. I could not quite remember his face. That, or I blurred him with his father, also thin, also with these problems, also called Aurel.

I had wanted this outing to be another apprehension, a lifting, especially after the death of my father. Instead, I'd ruined it with the churnings of my heavy mind.

21

Obituaries for William Foran, published in Ottawa newspapers in 1945, make no mention of freckles. The photos are
too faded to confirm or deny this bodily feature. The tributes
focus instead on your great-grandfather's fifty-two years with
the Public Service Commission of Canada, including as secre-
tary to Prime Minister Wilfrid Laurier, and his involvement in
founding the Stanley Cup in the early twentieth century, a cup
eventually awarded annually to the best team in the National

Hockey League. "Billy" Foran, as friends called him, also served as an alderman and school trustee, and as commissioner for the Capitals Lacrosse Club. He fathered two daughters and three sons: "Mrs. A.J. LaRochelle, Mrs. Frank Callaghan, William Henry, John A., and Charlie J." His wife, and mother to the five children, was Susan Francis McGrady, and William Foran's own parents are given as John Foran and Alice Hickey, late of Quebec City. William Foran is praised in one obituary as "a sterling citizen, and a man with an incredibly large number of friends." In another he is described as someone "gifted with an Irish wit and pleasant manner" who was "extremely popular" throughout the Civil Service. He died at seventy-four. No cause of death is given.

The little boy carrying the teddy bear is your grandfather, aged two or three. The year would be around 1911. Again, there is no way of telling if he had freckles, neither from this image nor from any others you have found. Based on your vague memories of sitting in his lap as a child, and on portrait shots later in life, he did not. All these photos are from the albums you and your sister were given after Shirley Foran died in 2016. You started going through the faded and damaged materials in earnest in 2019—in preparation for this book. The images of Charlie Foran in uniform intrigue you. One shows him feeding pigeons in Trafalgar Square in London. The other has him walking on a street with Ruthie Foran, your grandmother. You noticed these two photos immediately and tried getting your

father to examine them more closely during his first—and only—look at the albums. Based on Colonel Foran's uniform, were they not possibly taken on the same day? Meaning Ruthie *was* in London during the war, and did see her husband during those seven years he was absent? Meaning that, during the period your father and aunt were taken away from Ruthie because, they were told, she was "sick" with alcoholism, she was on a boat to England to visit her husband? Lt. Col. Charlie Foran would have had the status and authority to arrange such a visit. Among the papers are clippings from newspapers in 1945–46 concerning C.J. Foran's work as first "embarkation commandant, south coast ports," and later "port commandant" in charge of bringing troops back from Europe. He is described as "the man responsible for loading both military and civilian passengers—and the world's largest liner [the *Queen Elizabeth*] carries about 13,000 each trip." In 1946 he saw Winston Churchill off from Southampton, introducing "Good Old Winnie," as the crowd called him, to the commander of the liner that would transport the former—and future—prime minister safely across the Atlantic, bound for New York.

Again, the photos are faded, and don't make manifest what you know to be true: your rust-haired father had freckles over his body, including clusters beneath his eyes. You note how many surviving images from his childhood are taken in snow, reflecting Ottawa's climate, and how few—none that you are aware of, to be exact—show your father with his own

father. Below are two photos set in deliberate juxtaposition. One is your parents on their wedding day in 1955. As well as evidencing the color of his hair and freckled face, the photo is notable for *not* featuring your grandfather. Charlie Foran, by then a businessman, horseman and husband to Shirley, drove nine hours to attend his son's wedding in Blind River, and

later gave the newlyweds airplane tickets to New York and a week at the Astoria hotel as wedding gifts. What he could not give his only son, apparently, was love and attention. Nor did he do anything to encourage the compassion that accompanies security and well-being, and discourage the sour, small, defeating meanness that causes quiet but permanent damage, especially in children. Finally, because the photos were hers, and because she loved your grandfather for a quarter century and then mourned him another forty years, here is Shirley, with her beloved, celebrating a good day at the races in 1963. Charlie Foran died on November 28, 1973, age sixty-four, of cancer. You confirm that with several sources: cancer, not heart disease.

Below is the photo your family wanted for the newspaper obituary that you wrote for your father. The resolution wasn't high enough. Here it is anyway, showing the red hair, the everywhere freckles, the mischievous smile and, perhaps, underlying shyness. Less evident is any resemblance to his own father. Maybe he looks more like his grandfather, William Charles?

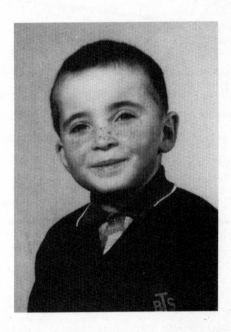

And who's this? You note the freckle Band-Aid across the nose, even in the five-year-old. And those are his ears, high forehead, lips and smile. Since his death, the generational collapse has accelerated: you wear his body armor of freckles, move with his short-legged walk. Snore the same, sneeze the same, same grunts, harrumphs, vocal tics. There are other resemblances and echoes yet to be discovered, no doubt.

The dissolve, the instability, continues.

22

If fortune, it ever should favor me
And I to have money in store
I'll come back and I'll wed the wee lassie I left
On Paddy's green shamrock shore

TRADITIONAL

The Foran family descends from the Ó Fuartháin clan, sometimes spelt Ó Fuaráin. In Irish *fuar* means cold and *fuarán* is a
spring or pool. My father's people—what little I knew of them—
were too busy feuding with, and damaging, each other to pay
attention to their ancestors, and as a result I grew up with
nothing more than vague lore about previous generations.
Nor was I raised gaudily Irish Canadian: no rebel songs sung
over whiskey, no recitations of poems by Yeats, no fake family
crests on walls. I took my cues from my father who, ruddy hair
and flaring temper aside, was most "Irish" in his learned and
unrelenting critique of the British—both British empire and,
frankly, British essence, manifested locally in the Orange
Order, bullyboys for the perpetration of old-world bigotry and
colonial kitsch. It was only many years after I had left home,

had my own family and was confronting his death that the photo album left behind by my grandfather's second wife compelled me to learn more about those diaspora O Fuarthains.

I went online and quickly learned a lot. For instance: the Forans favored the United States, United Kingdom, France and Canada as their destinations of exile. No surprise there. But where they settled within those countries was striking. Two cities dominated in North America: the Ottawa region in Canada and Milwaukee in the United States. Milwaukee, it turned out, had been fast becoming an Irish-American epi-center, until an accident in September 1860. Seven hundred mostly Irish immigrants had traveled by steamship down Lake Michigan for a day in Chicago. On their return home in a gale that same night, the vessel was rammed by a schooner and broke apart, drowning nearly half the passengers. The city's Third Ward, where the Irish had only just established their new lives, was devastated.

My wife, Mary, is from Milwaukee. We met in graduate school in Dublin, where we were both studying, among other writers, William Butler Yeats and Samuel Beckett. Her mother was born a Corrigan—from *corragan*, Irish for pointed—and her large Catholic family has deep roots in the city of her birth. Gathered in a bar especially, her people manifest an Irish-American exuberance straight out of the movies, albeit with less punching.

Parallel to my late-midlife interest in genealogy was the renewal of an earlier preoccupation with traditional music, traceable back to the trip to Ireland I'd made as a teenager. From the moment I did not fall from a cliff on the Aran Islands, I'd been absorbed by the music emerging over the centuries from this country with the same determination as its inhabitants fled. Immigration songs, especially, held me the way the sky beyond the precipice at Dún Aengus held those idling seagulls within its blue draft—in flight, yet not moving. For forty years I listened to songs of human flight and melodies of forced motion as though they must contain clues to my own history, my own identity. And in the year after my father's passing, I listened more closely still.

"Paddy's Green Shamrock Shore" had been the first song to hold me in its draft back in 1979. A young man has boarded a ship on Derry quay, one bound for New York. The song gives a month of departure—late May, after the worst of winter weather—but not a year. It also provides travel details. While in port, the boat takes on five thousand gallons of drinking water, enough for an Atlantic crossing. Nearly all the passengers get seasick soon after departure, and are confined to their bunks, where they pine for their families and lovers and make new friends. The unnamed narrator is also lovesick, declaring over and over his intention to return to his sweetheart, identified as Liza, once he has earned his fortune in America. At the docks on Manhattan Island, he and his mates are to be separated, likely to pay off their passages. They drink a parting glass, in case they, too, never see each other again.

They may not. America is sprawling; most jobs for immigrant men are dangerous. Nor is it likely the narrator is reunited with "Liza dear," or Derry town. He could die building the Erie Canal or laying railway lines out west. If the boat is crossing the ocean during the Civil War, he might already have traded passage for service in the Union army. He could be enlisted on the docks, provided a uniform and rifle, and sent to a battlefield, where he takes a bullet in the chest—all in the space of a few weeks. Less tragically, he might meet an American girl within that same time frame, and rudely drop the one back home.

As for Liza, she may never learn what became of her true love. Does she remain faithful regardless, spinsterhood and lonely old age her reward? Or, after a period, does she too move on and marry another boy, raise a family with him instead? Here is a different song, one equally plaintive: a young woman in the nineteenth century has her own precariousness to negotiate. Dry land in Ireland keeps a body from drowning, but not much else. There is little by way of education or dignified employment. There are waves of typhus and cholera. There is malnutrition and even starvation, although this version of the song does not reference the Great Famine of 1845–50. But the tune doesn't need additional details of woe to relay the poignancy of the lot of ordinary folks. It has a melody for that purpose, and the tune is as inconsolable as it is gorgeous, a raw, bright keen.

The gorgeous tune and essential story of "Paddy's Green Shamrock Shore" are as commonplace as birdcall and as eternal as sunrise. Thousands are sailing, or flying, or crossing borders on foot. We were then, we are now. In the Bible, the book of Genesis is followed by Exodus. According to these narratives, humanity was born in a garden. Not long after, we started relocating, sometimes coerced into moving, nearly always under duress. Accompanying the migrations has been the singing of songs along the road. These songs tell our tales and confess our yearnings, fears and heartbreaks, of which there are no end. They also convey in their melodies our sweetness and sensitivity, the way the beauty and brutality of the world rubs us raw. Must they be mostly sad? What a question.

At the outset, Irish music alone captivated me: Donegal fiddle tunes and Clare piping, harp melodies composed in the eighteenth century and traditional bands that played with the ferocity of the Clash. But then I discovered Québécois button-accordions and fiddlers out of Cape Breton, work songs from the Hebrides and Breton sea shanties. A portal opened, and over the decades it has kept widening: Appalachian folk songs and Afro-Cuban jazz; griots and kora from West Africa; Agadez guitars and Congotronics; fado from the Azores and rai from Algeria. Any music that retells Genesis followed, often enough, by Exodus, and then the new garden, the fresh flight.

Love and death, faith and acceptance run through the lyrics. The melodies, wherever they start from, share other qualities as well. Song structures are repetitive. Tunes catch hold and won't let go. Minor keys dominate, and there is occasional dissonance, but always the hunger is for resolution and harmony. Much of the music is made for dancing, and the steps, unfamiliar at first, are easy to learn. If not for dancing, the songs are for singing or humming along to. The singing, playing, humming, dancing—these are being done every day in bars or coffee houses or places of worship in Bamako, Dublin, Algiers, Cardiff, Cape Town, New Orleans, Poughkeepsie, Sarnia, Glasgow, Trois-Rivières.

A final quality these songs and tunes share is that many are credited to "Anonymous" or "Traditional." They aren't by me—or any "me" that anyone can remember, after a point—and they aren't by you. They are by us.

This music, I decided when I began to listen to it again, listening now as a fifty-eight-year-old, registering the notes—or perhaps the full melody—of primordial loss in his life, is a wooden ship crossing an ocean. On deck stands a woman, clothes ragged and hair unwashed, savoring her allotted thirty minutes of fresh air and sunlight. She hears the rigging creak and feels the hull pitch, as though cradled by a reckless deity. Not knowing where to settle her gaze without suffering nausea, she closes her eyes, worrying her rosary beads and turning her thoughts away from the image of the boat cracking open while she plummets into the depths. What of her parents back home? What of the boy awaiting her on the far shore? Thinking about them doesn't help either. The woman hums a tune instead, tapping her foot to "The Butterfly," a slip jig meant to capture a butterfly in flight. Next, she sings "Donal Og," so softly it could be mistaken, especially as she works the beads, for muttered prayer. She learned the song from her grand-mother, dead these long years. How she misses her gran. How she misses being a child watching a butterfly, or two butter-flies, weaving through a glade of flowers, stopping to drink the nectar. The woman hears the singing voice of her mother's mother in her own, especially the thin vibrato, infused with pride and natural heartbreak, and wonders where she is now, and will they truly be reunited, and isn't life a sad thing, a wak-ing dream, so quickly come and gone.

Postscript: "Donal Og" is ancient. It can be played as a melody but is best sung, especially in the original Irish. Unusually for a well-known piece, "The Butterfly" has a composer and a prob-able date of composition. Dubliner Tommie Potts is widely believed to have written it in the 1950s. As such, the woman on board the ship could not have been humming that tune—or not exactly. But she would have hummed one quite like "The Butterfly," which is, after all, quite like hundreds of other slip jigs in the repertoire. And these days, fewer and fewer musi-cians who perform the melody know about anyone named Tommie Potts. They assume it is by "Traditional"—by "us."

> Black as the slow is the heart inside me
> Black as the coal with the grief that drives me
> Black as the boot print on shining hallway
> 'Twas you that blackened it ever and always

For you took what's before me and what's behind me
You took east and west when you would not mind me
Sun, moon and stars from you have taken
And Christ likewise if I'm not mistaken

My Donal Og, when you sailed over the water

23

One year almost to the day after my father's death, I had work done on my heart. The cardiologist who'd decided I "didn't look right" earlier in the autumn had made the correct call. Thanks to him, further tests revealed advanced angina that could not be fixed with aspirin and lifestyle changes. And because of his diagnosis, I likely skirted having a major heart attack and (had I survived) a double bypass.

Instead, I underwent two angioplasty procedures spaced over twenty-one days. The procedures confirmed that my two largest arteries had calcified and narrowed 80 and 90 percent respectively. Angioplasty is minimally invasive and routine enough. It is also a startling bodily intrusion. A catheter tube is inserted into an artery, either at the groin or, in my case, in an incision at the right wrist. The tube travels up the arm to the chest, its progress tracked on an MRI. Once the scan identifies the narrowed coronary artery, doctors thread a deflated balloon up the tube. Water is pumped in. The balloon inflates at the narrowed point, expanding the artery back to its proper size. If the artery is severely damaged, doctors next recommend the insertion of a metal tube, called a stent, to prop up the walls. Assuming the patient agrees to this on the spot, the same balloon carries the stent from wrist to blockage. Balloon and wire are then withdrawn. The stent, however, stays. And holds. For good. For—it is hoped—the duration.

Most angioplasty procedures end with a stent or two being inserted. I required five stents to keep my arteries open—a lot, the doctors agreed, and too many for one session. After the second procedure, I left the hospital with a vision in my head of five very small, very muscled miners keeping the roof of a mineral seam they were working from collapsing onto them. Their arms trembled from the strain and their faces were contorted purple and pink.

Seven months later, one of the stents did collapse. I had felt it coming for weeks beforehand, could even point to where around my heart at least one of the miners lay interred under rubble. There was another procedure and, sure enough, doctors had to re-stent. I now had a medical condition known as "re-narrowing." The diagnosis wasn't happy, but so long as there were warnings, and I heeded them, and there was time enough to intervene with more angioplasty, the doctors could keep fixing the problem. An ultrasound was performed, and I lay on my side watching my five-stented heart on a monitor. I could scarcely believe the sight. An ugly, pulpy mess trapped in a cavity, it was pumping away, a spastic thwomp, thwomp, thwomp, like an animal gone berserk from confinement. When the technician affirmed what I already knew—the heart did this all day, all night, every day, every night, no breaks, no time off—I let out the sigh of, in effect, a lifetime. Who can keep such a pace? Already tired, maybe for the previous several years, I grew weary just looking at it—me? us?—on the screen. Better to turn away.

I no longer had a strong heart. I had one perhaps grown weary. It seemed I also had a broken heart, although not from love, and medicine was ready and willing to keep on doing the mending. Medicine had better keep on the mending; time alone wasn't going to heal this kind of broken. Nonetheless, I didn't have a heavy heart and was not faint of it. Mine was bleeding, sure—but it always had been. And acute coronary disease or not, it was rarely sick or sinking; if anything, it was perpetually inclined to leap and sing. Skipping a beat was a routine occurrence, as was swooning, swelling, melting, softening. With passion came fleeting sensations of burning and being on fire, of crying out. Without passion came spells of feeling poor and pitiful, lonely and blue. Better that than having a lying or cheating one? I trusted so. My heart had never been inclined to lay itself bare to either friends or strangers and had only infrequently responded with the buoyancy of youth. It was naturally soft, incapable of fully hardening against anyone. Does that mean it was never cold or calculating? It does not. I lacked the heart to be cruel, even to be kind, and occasionally wore mine on my sleeve. For some, that was an indicator of sentimentality and sloppiness; for others, of openness, being in the right place. Okay to all that. But was my heart truly brave? I couldn't say. Was it authentically kind?

Again, not my call. But now that I thought on it, had I ever known its contents? Had I known what it wanted, needed, desired; what it was after, set on, would do it a world of good? And had I listened to it, followed it, crossed it in times of peril, just in case? Had I taken adequate care of it/us? Apparently not. Had I taught it—or it taught me—how to love, be loved, show love, know love, take love in, keep love safe and lock it away? I was pretty sure I *had* kept my heart near and dear, and although mine wasn't made of gold—show me one of those!— neither was it of stone. A confession: I did wish my own was lighter, a born keeper of light. It wasn't, but neither did it welcome, nor often recognize, the dark. I wished as well that I understood why some people say it can be a window. A window onto what? A heart doesn't open out.

I peeked at that monitor again: my heart sat wedged in an airless space, a darkened chamber, and seemed to be working itself—how else to put this?—to death.

After the three angiograms and five stents, I knew one thing for certain—I had a heart that was talking like never before. Here are some of its louder conversations.

Music. I hear it differently now. With music I love, I hear it for the first time each time I listen, as though one of us is brand new. Arrangements of notes I may have known for a half century have become fresh astonishments—their structures, colors, emotions, assertions, resonances. Also, their silences, hymns, it is clear, to a much louder quiet encircling this sound and sensation. Assuming the reel, fugue, air, concerto, song, motet or drone has long been banked in the auditory cortex of my brain, the sounds must be activating another region these days. Casual listening is no longer possible. I hear every note, and immediately feel it going to work, working me over, even—does this make sense?—pulling it/me/us away. The music could be "Row, row, row your boat" or the first movement of Bach's keyboard Concerto no. 5, Toumani Diabaté's "Elyne Road" or Martin Hayes's version of "The Butterfly." Or a thousand, ten thousand, other pieces. Before them all, I feel alert and open.

Animals. I am seeing animals anew as well. I am noticing them and am astonished. Animals, it turns out, surround me constantly, on the ground, in the water, moving through the air, and view these spaces as theirs too—territory, community, home. How busy they are. How full their lives. These days, if I pass a human and a dog on a sidewalk, I am likely to linger over the dog, wonder how they are doing, if their environment is caring. I think back on animals that lived under the same roof as me, that I once imagined I "owned." When our girls were young, we had two cats. Orlando and Reilly were brothers, gray-and-white tabbies, one long haired, the other short, and they graced our house for a decade, their personalities as distinct from each other as Anna's from Claire's. I don't own my children, and never have. How could I have believed I held dominion over Orlando and Reilly, except by coercion? And it was only their bodies I could ever possess, never their spirits. I am stupefied that I did not reflect on these hierarchies sooner.

It is a stark failure to live up to the task that Einstein outlined: "to free ourselves from this prison by widening our circles of compassion to all living beings and the whole of nature." I recently sent one daughter an article I had read on humans' evolving understanding of the lives of animals. Anna replied, *This understanding also breaks down walls we've set up between humans and animals, who share a kind of fundamental conscious- ness, but are perhaps separated by this notion of metacognition.*

Loved ones. I look more closely at them now, my wife, our children, my widowed mother, siblings and old friends. I observe, and work at registering these observations, staying with the thoughts. I focus on my loved ones' faces, linger on their expressions and gestures, ask them to repeat words I have not quite taken in. I try, try, try not to be so perpetually distracted—as if I've suddenly gone off medications that kept me jittery for a half century. Did I live for that long without fully being in any moment? Never mind that the moment would not, could not, last nor be replicated, and so, no, of course I shouldn't put off being right here, right now, with these people I cherish. Mary, for instance, whom I met when I was twenty-three, will casually raise her legs up behind her head while lying on the couch, like a baby wishing to converse with its toes. She does so now, in her late fifties, and has been doing so, she informs me tartly, the entire time I have known her. How is it possible that I have never noticed this before? But mercifully, here she still is, my wife of thirty- plus years, and here they mostly still are, daughters, siblings, friends. How beautiful their features and smiles, the light and lift, sadness and play, in their eyes. How beautiful their aging bodies and spirits.

Tears. In his final years my father would well up when he was in company, and sometimes with me. He would go quiet, gaze straight ahead, expression inward and eyes gauzy. If tears trickled down his cheeks, family members pretended not to notice. He would raise a fist to hastily wipe them clear. He and I never discussed the tears, and I dared not presume to know why he wept—or if he had any idea himself. But since the stents, I have likewise struggled, and naturally I have ideas about why. Loved ones trigger these tears—those beautiful faces, voices, smiles—but so do music and animals, leaf storms in autumn and ponds of summer lilies, cedar trees swaying in high winds and gardens loud with birdcall. It has long been my nature to be awed by most things; now, it seems my nature to be grateful for them. I am in love, and I love all that vanishes. And at such moments of awe, humility, ardor, awareness, I am foremost grateful for the metacognition that perhaps separates me from the rest of the planet's nonhuman inhabitants—the roaring sentience I have often lamented and sought escape from. The world I have briefly inhabited, and *known* myself to be briefly inhabiting, is well worth weeping over.

24

Here is a scene. You stand on a street in a remote mountain village. It is a June morning, and you have just had breakfast with your wife in the only restaurant open that early. She has returned to the motel to pack up. You are considering a walk down to the lake. On holiday, you are passing through this place for the first, and probably only, time in your life. The setting is spectacular, town and lake cupped by mountains like water in the palm of the Buddha's hand. But your focus is caught by the century-old building the restaurant occupies. A former bank, the building has apartments on its second floor. One apartment is accessed by a wooden exterior staircase. A woman about your age—two months shy of fifty-nine— is climbing down the stairs. Something about her face in profile, how she loops errant hairs behind her ear, is familiar. You watch her, wondering where and when you could have met. At the bottom step, she turns toward the street and, spotting you, smiles politely, the way one does with strangers.

Your entire body reacts, from the knees up. In your stomach, a flip. In your neck, a pulse. In your mouth, a dryness like when confronting danger—at cliff's edge, say, the path treacherous. Above all, in your heart there is a jolt, a jump, along with a flash burn across the chest. These are not good sensations. Recently you've had your heart repaired, and there are signs you will need further work.

Your expression must be showing an array of emotions, none of them appropriate: astonishment, confusion, fright, pride, tenderness, along with a love impossible to hide or disguise.

The woman, who could easily retreat up the stairs, crosses the lawn. "Are you okay?" she says.

Her voice is her voice. Her eyes are her eyes. Her smile is her smile, but also that of her ancestors, based on family photos you have seen—tentative and apologetic, under-written, faintly, by sadness. You had always worried about that family trait in her; had been, as a matter of fact, worrying about it recently. This was probably not good for your heart either.

"The bench," you say.

She guides you to a bench.

"You look like you might fall over," she says.

"I feel that way," you admit. "Fall right off a cliff."

She is silent.

Of course she would end up in a village in the mountains. As a teenager and then a young adult, she balked at cities, and talked of living in the country, cherishing animals as much as humans. She also launched a career raising awareness about the climate emergency, being part of the solution, not the problem. Of late you have been thinking about that too: how life might play out for her; how, given her nature, she can best secure happiness and fulfillment. The trick, you believe, is to understand sadness differently, especially as you age. You've been reading about this and can't wait to share what you've been thinking with her.

"Can you sit?" you say. "Just for a second."

She sits with her usual grace, although her shoulders now droop, like her mother's did. She also lays a hand on the wood slats between you, marking a line that should not be crossed.

It's true—you are desperate to touch her.

"You have cats?" you ask, indicating the apartment. "And a dog?"

She blinks yes and yes.

"I figured you would. You were so passionate."

"Pardon me?"

"You loved Orlando and Reilly."

Frown lines cross her forehead. You remember the lines, or the beginnings of them, from when she was a beautiful child, and struggled to sleep, nightmares spooling on an old film projector behind her eyelids. She has settled into a deeper beauty in late middle age: the mouth, cheekbones, eyes, hair. You had guessed this would happen as well.

"Those cats were part of our family," you say. "They shared our lives. We shouldn't have given them away when we moved. It was a mistake. I never stopped regretting it."

"I'm sorry," the woman says. "Do we know each other?"

You have no answer. "I've been reading a lot of Rilke," you say. "Rainer Maria Rilke. A German poet from the early twentieth century. Very influential, especially after his death."

"Thanks for the lesson."

A bad habit, and one both daughters, and your wife, tease you about: Dad talks; Dad lectures; mansplaining. Your father was the same.

"Rilke talks about how sadness can be a sign that a transformation is under way," you say nonetheless. "When sad, we're actually experiencing 'moments of tension,' our emotions attempting to speak, although they are in shock and naturally shy. It's why we often go quiet and inward. Rilke says we should be open to sadness, try to understand it as how the future is coming into us, showing us a way to connect, to be ready for what comes next."

"Did you hit your head?"

"I didn't hit my head."

"Were you in an accident?"

"I had five stents put in my heart," you say. "Though that's not what you are asking."

"I have to go," she says, standing up. "Someone is waiting for me."

With her eyes she indicates the staircase. A moment earlier you glimpsed another woman in a bay window on the second floor, watering plants on a sill. The glass refracts much of the light. But you did discern that this woman is aged, and tall, and has curly hair and the posture of a wilted flower. Her outline alone, the curls, make your heart—no other way to put it—burst. The math works; her mother lived to ninety-six. Also, she never smoked, exercised daily and looked after herself. Aged sixty, she could raise her legs over her head and count her toes.

Your own legs will not hold your weight. It is for the best; otherwise, you might try following her late-middle-aged daughter across the lawn. "Before you go," you say. "Can I say one thing?"

Being kindly—she always was—she shrugs, lets the deranged person go on a little longer.

"My dad, your grandfather, gave *me* a look the final time I saw him alive. The expression tore me up with regret. And I don't want that for you. I want you to see me now, and know I am happy and full of gratitude. All along I've felt loved and been able to give love in return. That's it," you add, dropping your gaze to the ground. "That's pretty much the whole show."

She pauses, then thinks better of engaging further. She speaks while walking. "Are you aware that you just used the word 'regret' twice in thirty seconds?"

At that, you smile, knowing that she gets it, or is starting to. "Keep walking," you say. "Let Rilke explain."

You quote from memory:

"Once for each thing. Just once; no more. And we too,
Just once. And never again. But to have been
This once, completely, even if only once;
To have been at one with the earth, seems beyond undoing."

"That's beautiful," she says. Looping strands of graying hair around her ear, she climbs the stairs to rejoin her mother.

~

Here is another scene. You are paging through a family photo album that belonged to your grandfather's second wife. You are doing so in a spacious room, formerly a stand-alone coach house, which you and your wife recently attached to the main house. The home, made of powdery red brick local to the area, dates from around 1870; the coach house might be older. Though you pretend otherwise, you are scouring the faded and dissolving photos in search of a family member who has your face. Once before, you came across a random daguerreotype from the 1860s that revealed a man who could have been you in the mirror, plus bushy mustache. But on this occasion, you are searching among actual ancestors, three generations' worth. And you have reason to be optimistic; your crowd did not marry widely outside their kind— A to B to A again in race, geography, religion. You must lurk somewhere among the faded Forans and Mortons, McGradys and O'Neils. Where else would you dwell?

You subscribe to an ancestry search engine, and a few minutes of research rewinds your family into the nineteenth century. About your great-grandfather, William Foran, you already know a fair amount, thanks to those print obituaries taped inside the photo albums, although it is good to be reminded that "Billy" was married for forty years to Susan McGrady, also of Ottawa. You meet for the first time Thomas Foran—your great-grandfather's dad—and your great-great-grandmother Alice Hickey. They were married in Ottawa in 1868, both aged twenty-three, but hailed, according to the certificate, from Quebec City. Alice's parents are given as Michael Hickey and Mary Burke; Thomas's are Michael Foran and Mary O'Neil. Previously you learned that your grandmother, Ruthie Foran, née Morton, had a mother who was likewise an O'Neil, Sarah Ann, better known as Daisy. She was from Dublin. Soon you are accustomed to a genealogy overrun by Annes and Margarets, Jameses and Johns. And there is certainly no escaping Marys.

But Michael Foran is the ancestor you wish to find. Your great-great-great-grandfather—also, it so happens, your actual brother, alive and well in northern Ontario in 2019—must have been the one who obtained passage on a ship. Likely he did so around 1840, and though he was probably driven out of Ireland by cholera, he had the good fortune to escape before hunger and disease took hold in 1845; the same year it seems, he and Mary O'Neil became parents in Ottawa. A million Irish died over the next sixty months, and a million more, mostly the poor, fled into exile. Michael may have emigrated with Mary or met her on the boat. Or perhaps they ran into each other during their early days here, at mass on Sunday or as domestics in a grand house.

You want to know more about his passage from Ireland to Canada. How Michael Foran managed those long weeks at sea. How he later understood the experience of migration. Learning about your ancestor's Atlantic crossing suddenly feels urgent, and a photo of him would, you believe, reveal what is essential. From one shore to another, with so much water in between; from one identity to another, with so many points of connection. Three to four weeks at sea, if the winds are decent; fifty-nine years trapped in a chest cavity—if the heart keeps on thwomping.

A thought comes to you. Couldn't Michael Foran have first entered Canada nearby Port Hope, the town near Toronto where you are examining those photo albums in your circa-1870 house? Many Irish did pass through this port before settling along the north shore of Lake Ontario. Suppose he took work on landing—he was likely penniless, and winter fast approaching—and wound up shoeing horses in an informal blacksmith's shop partway up the hill from the harbor? A small shop, built out of the local brick, known for being powdery, which was later converted to a coach house, and later again attached to the main building?

The conversation happens late one night when the sky is blacked out, and the wind hurls leaves against the windows.

"It's himself?" Michael Foran says.

"Is it?"

"Well, aren't you?"

"Maybe," you say.

"I think so."

"Then you are . . . ?"

Michael Foran smiles. A smile like your dad's, or maybe his dad's. Not like your own.

"Can I ask you about the journey?" you say.

"To get here?"

"Yes."

"This fancy house?"

"Across the ocean."

"You tell me."

"Sorry?"

"You made it, as well. Everyone does."

"Okay," you say. "But what I want to know most about is . . ." You scroll through your mental list, settling on two items. There is the devastation that comes from leaving loved ones behind: the curl of her hair, the slope of her shoulders. As well, the fear of the unknown future, one most likely dark. A bottomless well, an ocean deep.

"The girl I left behind?" Michael Foran guesses.

"Then there was a girl?"

"There's always a girl."

"But who is Mary O'Neil?"

"Ah," he says. "There's always a Mary too."

You wait.

"Met her on the boat. From another village, down in Cork. She's grand. No complaints at all, except her accent. I understand barely the half of what she says. Might be for the best," he adds with another grin.

"Okay."

"But come here a minute," Michael Foran says. "Let me tell you about the music that kept us from going mad those nights and days. It's what you want to learn, is it not?"

Is that true? What you really want is the music?

"There was a lad with a concertina, an O'Sullivan from Mallow, and a piper from Glengarriff. Singers too, of course, plenty of them. We had great times, singing and dancing—at least, when we weren't heaving our guts into slop pails or confined to bunks below."

His phrasing reminds you of a song. "Do you know 'Paddy's Green Shamrock Shore'?"

"How does it go?"

You hum the melody.

"Sing it for me."

You try:

"From Derry Quay, we sailed away
On the twenty-third of May.
We were boarded by a pleasant crew
Bound for Americay."

Michael Foran winces. "Sounds familiar. A stronger singing voice might help."

"The narrator leaves behind a girl named Liza. He vows to return and marry her once he's made his fortune."

"Does he promise that? Poor lad. Poor lass too—if she waited."

"What did you sing on the ship?"

"Here's one," he says. He sings, his voice high and lonesome and pitch-perfect.

> "Oh, the streams of Bunclody they flow down so free
> By the streams of Bunclody I'm longing to be
> A-drinking strong liquor in the height of my cheer
> Here's health to Bunclody and the lass I love dear."

"I guess there *is* always a girl," you say.

"This story takes a bad turn," Michael Foran says. He sings another verse, and then explains. "The girl comes from money, you see, 'a great store of riches and a large sum of gold.' But the boy has nothing. He abandons family and friends and everything he knows and loves, boards a packet-boat to cross a raging ocean, all in the faint hope of finding wealth enough to be a worthy match."

Closing his eyes to concentrate, your great-great-great-grandfather finishes the song:

> "So fare you well father and my mother, adieu
> My sister and brother farewell unto you
> I am bound for America my fortune to try
> When I think on Bunclody I'm ready to die."

You reflect on the lyrics. "Maybe the tale doesn't end so badly," you say. "Maybe the immigrant lucks into a good deal shortly after he settles in New York or Chicago, Ottawa or

Montreal. He earns a fortune, a small one, and writes home with a date of return. And then he shows up in Bunclody with his own riches and gold, marries the girl, and lives happily ever after?"

Michael Foran gives you a look, half pity, half disgust. "No chance of that happening," he says.

"None?"

"Not in this life. Not unless you're dreaming. It's like I tell my bairns. 'Wake up! Wake up! Don't sleep so much!'"

"*You* say that?" you say. "'Wake up! Wake up! Don't sleep so much!'?"

"I do. To my children—Thomas, and the others."

Your heart threatens to burst its cage, again. It was the music you wanted, after all. "It sure is a beautiful song," you say.

~

One of these scenes happened. The other hasn't—yet.

25

Dec 2019

Dear Dad,

I can't seem to finish this book.

Thirty-six months ago, I began thinking and writing about you dying, and the onset of sadness within me. I could not identify the task then, but now I suspect I was hoping to reconcile your mortality with the unsettling of my being. I made a list titled "Why Older People Get Sad," thinking I would be tracking these laments, one "why" at a time. Here is the original:

- Death of loved ones
- Loss of driving purpose: mating, children, career
- Ebbing of once vital relationships
- Overall feeling of diminishment—intellectual, creative, sexual
- Health issues
- Loneliness
- Pattern recognition in nature—i.e., mortality
- Tired of same old self

- Less and less taste to food
- Inability to find/feel/experience God

Now, much thinking and writing later, I have revised the list to make it truer to my real preoccupations and what I sensed coursing through these pages, half-formed and unresolved.

- Deepening awareness of the suffering and anxiety experienced by all humans
- Desire to help, see happy, those I care about
- Metacognition
- Superiority of music for expressing how it feels to be alive
- Clumsiness of words—my own, at least
- What Leonard Cohen said, words and music both perfect: "You lose your grip, and then you slip/into the masterpiece"
- Will miss everyone! Will miss everything!
- Our bodies
- Who we are until we are no longer
- The ultimate (nonhuman) nature of things

Perhaps the last three items require further explanation— all three because they are entwined. At first, I assumed it was your body, the obscure map outlined by the freckles along your arms, that I was exploring. But never has this book been only, or even principally, about you. Always the interrogation has been of my own body, the freckles that coat my arms too, from fingers to shoulders, and which are likewise an archipelago. And as for the notion that my inquiry was triggered by your slow decline, beginning three or four years ago? Living in Hong Kong during the tumult following 9/11, I wrote an essay about being far away from home at a moment when the planet started to spin faster. In the piece, I referenced the story of you shooting the bear, your father losing his nose in the Second World War, the tabernacle in our church with the mind shaft up to heaven, and Lao-Tzu wondering if he is a man dreaming that he is a butterfly, or the other way round. "To my father," I wrote then, "I should have said this: I don't miss the house I grew up in and I don't miss the basement where I watched TV. But I miss him, and have been lonely for him, on some strange, subterranean level, a current I am only now registering in the soles of my feet, only now beginning to feel rise up into my body, an ache that might just be the ache of loss, all my life."

We should have read that essay together when it was published in 2002, and we should have talked about it. Imagine: declaring in print that I was lonely for you and had been registering the loss of you all my life, while you were crafting birdcages and wandering hardware stores in happy retirement in Bobcaygeon. But I was on the far side of an ocean when the piece appeared and preoccupied with the death of a close friend. We Forans are timid people, passengers not only in our bodies but in the cargo vessel that conveys our emotions across those various seas, each container sealed, the contents frequently left to rot. Deflection, misdirection, sublimation: these are the tricks of the shy who are also the prideful, and the wounded who can't get their words right—not even close.

There is also the problem, expressed in number Nine on the revised list above, of who I have "been" while working on this book. "All over the map" would be one answer. "In perpetual motion" might be another. Better this: "Stepping into the river every day and never finding it the same. Stepping into the river and not remembering—until I reread my notes—that I had been there just twenty-four hours earlier." I dare an Atlantic crossing to reunite with my true love. I wait by the tree for Godot and do not move. I contain multitudes. I am a butterfly dreaming she is a woman. Which is true and which truth will more likely hold up? Which story is better told, which list most tightly crafted, to withstand the insecurities of self and the inexorable passage of time? Not me, not mine.

As for the final item—this declaration in black and white about the nature of the world—it, too, may be a thought I am only now beginning to engage. Early in the writing process I noticed that thinking about change and mutability was not compounding the midlife sadness I was feeling. Quite the opposite. Such moments of connection, however fleeting, and of apprehension, however imperfect, were offsetting those feelings—banishing them for a spell, reframing their underlying anxieties as silly and a waste. Such moments marked times when I voluntarily looked up, raised my line of sight. They were when I allowed the notion that human nature is *not* nature enough, not even close, to upend my too-conventional assumptions and preoccupations, free them for just long enough. Our lives play out adjacent to those rivers or nestled in those woods, the air either scorching or frigid, the light diffused by foliage or shade. However immersive, this topography and weather represent only the bottom tier of a canvas of clouds, skies and heavens. Above us lies fuller, deeper nature, most of which we can't discern—too-thick clouds and skies too-hazy, cold on our skins and burning in our hearts. We do not often experience the empyrean. Instead, we tell ourselves that we dwell in an entirely separate space, and are special, exempt. *That* delusion may be our greatest sadness, not to mention a pending disaster for the planet. Like many forms of decentering, apprehensions and liftings may serve to make us feel not so separate from the rest of things, not so reckless and restless, solipsistic and lonely. They may offer a welcome break from being who we usually are.

The tenth preoccupation on the new list could also be why I'm unable to finish this book. Regardless of a tightening chest as I sit at my desk, I can't yet absorb, never mind frame, this latest notion or get enough of my words to line up with sufficient elegance to cover the gaping holes, the embarrassing inadequacies, the not-even-understanding-what-I don't-understand, of my careening thoughts. The only way to stop unraveling the text is to quit it.

Is it enough to understand now *why* I have written this, even if I do not know how to—or if I should—complete the work?

I hope so.

I think of two further details from the period after your death, one a confession, the other a proclamation. Using my iPhone, I snapped photos of your corpse in the hospital bed a half hour after your spirit departed. Five images in all, each one appalling: teeth out of your head and mouth gaping, no sheet to cover your naked torso. With the machines already gone—the security team, the hired muscle, had abandoned the fearless leader seconds after he breathed his last—I could take my morbid time. Your left arm lay exposed, and I studied it, as interested in the IV bruises at the inner elbow as the freckles running to the wrist. The freckles too were washing away, a child's treasure map drawn on a sandy beach, the evening tide rolling in. I did not bother photographing them.

And the strangest part of my behavior? I stored the images on my phone, buried among tourist snaps from Tanzania and Australia and our home renovation. Months and months went by during which I neither glanced at your death mask nor remembered that I had access to it. Then I would come upon the five images by accident and be aghast and dismayed and wonder what was wrong with me. Vowing to delete them, I would take a final look, lingering. Then I would leave them on the phone and pretend I was simply not deciding what to do yet.

While you, who demanded to be cremated, were in an urn on the mantelpiece in your wife's living room.

I am clicking delete now. As I write this. One, two, three, four, five—the photos, vanished.

Now the proclamation.

A few weeks after you died, forty friends and family gathered to celebrate your life. It was a brutal late December day, the air infused with a primordial fear—of exposure, death by cold—that unsettled any who were obliged to breathe it in. Many of the guests interrupted their holidays to drive for hours over icy country roads to attend. Debbie delivered a moving elegy, and Michael was a welcoming host. Our mother, your spouse of sixty-two years, cried and laughed in equal measure at the fuss being made. No one from the Foran side of the family came, but there were several of Mom's relations, a handful of old friends or their middle-aged children, along with neighbors from the street where we grew up, colleagues from your office, people from the town where you retired. The party carried on from the church back to the house, and all agreed that you would have been mortified—if very pleased—by the attention. Also by the affection, the love, so effortlessly shown.

I proclaim this: You were loved, Dave Foran, by all those who *could* love you. You were dear to them and stayed in their hearts. You were well sent off.

Now I want to do the same. Here is how I imagine you might wish to end. Here is how I might wish to as well.

~

The woods are dark and quiet. Emerging from them, pheasant snares and traplines for rabbits laid out, you stand at the edge of a field carpeted in spring flowers. Mosquitoes buzz around your head and the brook you have stepped through fills your ears. The Winchester 44-40 rests in your arms. Someone, something, is moving in and out of trees across the clearing, a silhouette against an unstable backdrop. Instinctively, you nestle the rifle butt into your shoulder and rest two fingers on the trigger guard, the barrel still lowered. You scan for movement, squinting at the dawn light and sniffing at the air, walk a few paces until the brook is no longer a sound. All you see are birds darting from tree to tree, the foliage not yet filled in. All you smell are those flowers and the thawed earth, the perfume of cedar and spruce. But there is a bear on the far side of the field—there must be—and you may soon have to cause it harm, end its one wild and precious life. You have no wish to do this and do not, *do not*, think of your father, and whether he would approve of your courage. You think only of the animal across the field, and that you had best be fully awake—Wake up! Wake up!—to this gorgeous and clarified moment.

The house is cool and shaded. You lie in a bed on the second floor. Loved ones, cherished ones, are close by, on the far side of the wall or down a set of stairs. They have expressed their everlasting love through their gazes. They have done all they can and should be expected to do no more. At your insistence—kind insistence, you believe, and merciful—they have left you alone: to be here, now, and not miss a thing. The bedroom has a high ceiling and shelves lined with books, a bay window that cants light across the floor in geometric shapes. With the windows open, sounds enter as well. Across the street is an elementary school, its playground out front. Every morning at drop-off and recess, for an hour at lunch and another hour during pickup, the playground floods with children. This is what you cannot miss. The kids shout and sing, their voices tremulous, filled with trills, pips, shrieks and squeals. The sounds enter the room. They surround your bed. They slowly fill—or do they help empty?—your head.

Either way, you begin to drift, to lift, a long climb into the sky, that spiral of paint, making of you—you suppose—a bright white light. It might even read:

> To drift, to lift
> A long climb
> Into the sky
> That spiral of paint
> A bright white light of yourself.

Or not. After all, you are just one more worn-out body, one more mind seeking to be free of fever, right up until the last breath, and counting on the world's music to sing you out.

Charlie

ACKNOWLEDGEMENTS

Many readers will recognize snippets of well-known prose and poetry running through these pages. Certain poems and song lyrics, prose passages and lines from plays, have lodged in my memory over the past sixty or so years, and inflected, informed my thinking and expressing in ways I can scarcely account for. In this regard, all the words are closer to melodies or prayers. I hum them, chant them, even dance to them—so long as no one is looking.

Loudest, if still badly, hummed are the poems of W.B. Yeats, Mary Oliver, Emily Dickinson, Rumi, Rainer Maria Rilke, Dylan Thomas and E.E. Cummings, the prose of Heraclitus, Seneca, Marcus Aurelius, Anton Chekhov, Samuel Beckett and Annie Dillard, the songs of Leonard Cohen, Paul Simon and, of course, the composer known as Traditional. Quite likely there are other melodies being prayed in *Just Once, No More*, of which I'm not yet quite aware. Readers are invited to flag them if I've missed someone obvious.

Aislinn Hunter encouraged and enriched this book, helping me understand both the "why" and the "how" to make it better. Lynn Henry was no less supportive of my meanderings, patient as they followed their various, often dead-end, directions, and so attuned to the project I often felt she saw it more clearly—and may still. Yann Martel served as an early reader. Mary Ladky did the same, her twelfth such assignment, at the very least. Mary Ladky also listened, also as usual, to my end-of-day mumblings, and in this instance did much of it under the extra duress of pandemic confinement. Anna Foran, Claire Foran, Muriel Foran and Debbie Makarenko displayed similar patience and support. Charlotte Gray and Vincent Lam kindly helped check facts. Thank you all.

ABOUT THE AUTHOR

Charles Foran has published twelve books. He has won awards for his fiction, non-fiction and journalism, and is a member of the Order of Canada. He lives in Toronto.